WEB TO SUCCESS

How to Become a Better You

JO BIRD

authorHOUSE®

AuthorHouse™ UK
1663 Liberty Drive
Bloomington, IN 47403 USA
www.authorhouse.co.uk
Phone: 0800.197.4150

Edited by Amber Krogh.

Published by AuthorHouse 11/18/2016

ISBN: 978-1-5246-6622-4 (sc)
ISBN: 978-1-5246-6623-1 (hc)
ISBN: 978-1-5246-6621-7 (e)

Library of Congress Control Number: 2016919022

Print information available on the last page.

This book is printed on acid-free paper.

Contents

About the author

Jo Bird is a wife and mother living with her family and two cats in the home counties of England. Jo has only recently come to realise, with help from a friend, that writing is the best way to share the wealth of experience she has gleaned from her years as a professional Project Manager and mentor to others. Jo began her career in Information Technology, moved on to Finance and then fell accidentally into Project Management. Over the years she's been formally taught a lot of tools and techniques but she firmly believes that experience is still the best way to learn and improve yourself. Her goal in life is to pass on as much of her experience as she can and give something back to the younger generation. It's her hope that they'll mature and then pass it on themselves, adding their own experiences into the pot. Jo is an empath, a mediator, and a natural optimist, always seeing the best in people. She never takes herself or life too seriously realising that life is too short and that laughter really does help. She's a control freak and everyone jokes about the number of lists she keeps in order to organise her life. Her own life experiences have taught her to follow her heart and never be afraid of emotion and as a result she's usually the shoulder to cry on for others. Jo is eternally grateful to all those who shared their knowledge and insight with her as she grew as a person. She truly believes that they are the reason she can now give back to the world by passing that knowledge on to the next generation.

Dedication

This book is dedicated to two dear friends. Without them it would never have happened. John Harris, who inspired, cajoled, pushed and forced me to write it in the first place. John also took to heart a lot of the messages, starting on his own journey to self-awareness, which motivated me even further. It was a roller coaster of a journey John, but we got there in the end, thank you so much. My great friend Amber Krogh. What can I say Amber, we haven't known each other very long but we connected instantly. You stuck by me, laughed with me through the good times and supported me through the bad times and ultimately edited the finished book. I couldn't have done this without you. Thank you so much, I love you both!

Introduction to developing success

'If you don't like something, change it. If you can't change it, change your attitude.' —Maya Angelou

I had a bit of a 'eureka' moment a while back. I came to realise that the mountain of information on positive thinking and personal development, I've collected over the years, is all interlinked. It's a whole spider's web, or network, of guidance, emotions, advice and development tools and techniques. Any one of these can be used in isolation, but they are much better when used together. As a whole they become a journey to a better you. That may not sound very enlightening to you but, since it was all drip fed to me over a period of many years, it was to me!

If you listen to studies, there are three things successful people do. They spend time getting to know themselves, self-awareness. They spend time improving themselves, personal development. They spend time

sharing themselves, emotional awareness. It's not an accident that these are the three sections of this book. These are the building blocks of success.

I've hoarded way too much information for me to put it all in here so I'm going to concentrate on self-awareness to start with as for me that embodies most of what goes into our potential for success. You'll also see a lot about negativity and positivity as that's key to helping us achieve our goals.

We control our own state of mind, no one else. We can decide to focus on what can bring us success. We don't need to be failing in our current lives in order to want to improve ourselves. We can choose to start each day with a positive frame of mind and decide to be enthusiastic, enjoy new ideas, challenges, and opportunities put in our way and look for success. If we understand that what we do will benefit us and others, then that motivates us. We can choose to smile and have a positive impact on those around us and generally enjoy our lives. Other people are not only affected by us, but they can affect our lives too and help us to succeed. We can go and seek out positive people. We can see them as assets adding value to our lives with their inputs, talents, and strengths rather than focussing on their weaknesses and what they can't do

As part of developing success and personal development we can use positive thinking and adopt a positive self-image. We should at least like what we see in the mirror, it's important. If we feel at any time that something we're doing is likely to fail we immediately put up barriers, it's only natural. In our modern, technology-filled, world we have to deal with an increasing amount of change. The important thing is to create a mindset to survive that change. Part of that mindset is the ability to be resilient. To bend instead of break. To persevere and adapt when faced with challenges. The same 'tools' help us to be more open and embrace new opportunities. This is more than a survival skill; it's learning to grow and growing to succeed. Self-awareness is just the starting block.

There's nothing more satisfying than knowing we can be resilient and agile, cope better with change, think positively, manage our emotions and stress, have a balanced life and make a positive difference around us. That's what self-awareness is all about. Some of you will be thinking that sounds easy and for some, it will be. For others, it's a struggle. I fall somewhere in the middle. There are parts where it was so obvious to me I wondered what all the fuss was about. Then I tried the stuff I personally find hard, and I realised I wasn't as self-aware as I thought I was. In fact, I was humbled. My big stumbling blocks are getting rid of my ego, forgiveness, expression of my emotions and time management. If you know me, you'll be chuckling to yourself because you'll have seen me struggle with all of them.

In 'real life' I come from a project management, I.T. (Information Technology) and finance background where, historically, it hasn't been the norm for these kinds of ideas to be widely disseminated. Fortunately, that has changed and is still changing. There's hope even for those of us stuck in the driest of careers. Some of us are trying to change it from within.

Some of what's in this book has been formally taught to me over the years, a lot of it comes from personal experience and my own take on life (which I admit can be quirky at best). There's a lot of myself in here, a lot of soul searching and emotion as to when and why I behave in certain ways. I've opened myself up, and I only hope I can reject ego, be self-aware enough and live up to my expectations at the end of it. This is written from my heart with honesty and integrity, and although the intention is to help you, there is also a bit of humour thrown in. This is my brain downloaded for your benefit and, in part, my way of giving something back.

I've included quotes at the beginning of each section which have all positively influenced me. Even if you don't read and take something from my thoughts and words then take something from those of others.

Enjoy!

Chapter 1

SELF-AWARENESS

'Fear comes from uncertainty; we can eliminate the fear within us when we know ourselves better.' —*Bruce Lee*
'To know oneself is to study oneself in action with another person.' —*Bruce Lee*

Definition of self-awareness

I thought I'd start with self-awareness. Actually, it's where I have to start. It's the cornerstone of everything else. Self-awareness is all about having a deeper understanding of ourselves, being aware of different aspects of ourselves and where we fall short, taking steps to discover ourselves and taking responsibility for our lives. It's a journey, in which we are the focus of attention; it's not a destination in itself. This journey pays attention to what we think, say, do, feel, eat and how we respond, react, decide and hide. It's all about looking down and observing ourselves from a higher viewpoint. It's the mirror on the ceiling of our bedroom! (I don't personally have such a mirror of course but if you do I won't judge you.) The way in which we act is influenced not just by our skill and knowledge but by our conduct and behaviour, our interaction with others, and our own needs. This is powerful stuff.

We're not born with self-awareness. It develops when we're very young, about a year old, it's self-awareness that is one of the first concepts of 'self' to develop. It becomes more developed by the time we reach about eighteen months old. It's central to each and every one of us, but it's not something of which we are consciously aware every moment of every day. If we were, we wouldn't find time for anything else. If you're anything like me, you do enough navel gazing as it is.

Self-awareness is the beginning of emotional intelligence (more about this later in personal development). It has nothing to do with being selfish! When we look at ourselves, does what we see meet our expectations? Does it align with what, or who, we want to be? It's about being positive, being consciously optimistic, taking personal responsibility, listening, challenging ourselves and learning from our mistakes.

Self-awareness can help if we want to know and understand more about ourselves and who doesn't? It can shed light on why we don't understand other people's reactions to 'stuff' we're doing or if we feel like we're weird or different, OK that's a big one for me! Feeling different has been a constant in my life, though not always in a bad way. It's a must if we want to be more confident or want higher self-esteem. Think about it. Is that you? If it is, read on.

People who are highly self-aware recognise their own strengths and weaknesses and understand where their talents can be best applied to deliver results or to achieve success. They're enthusiastic and positive, and they take responsibility for their own motivation. As a result, they can be truly inspirational to others. They understand that others have talents too and they appreciate the value they can add. They delegate effectively which helps others remain motivated and positive. They're able to adapt more easily to changes in their lives and they understand the need to behave in different ways according to a given situation because they're always aware of the impact of their behaviour on others. This may sound like the perfect human being, and it probably is. The reality is we will all sit somewhere on a sliding scale, and none of us will reach this level of perfection. Sigh! That doesn't mean we shouldn't try.

Self-awareness involves looking at our integrity, values, purpose, passion, and spirituality and forces us to acknowledge undefined areas of our life. It gives us a call to action. It can lead to simplification of our lives, removal of distractions, and focus on the present, letting go of ego, and acknowledging weakness. By becoming self-aware and understanding our strengths and limitations, we open up opportunities that aren't available

2

to us if we don't know ourselves. We're also able to have more honest and genuine relationships because the people that we're attracted to will be attracted to us for whom we really are. Wow! It doesn't get any better than that. I must have convinced you by now that this is worth a shot.

Having said all that, for those of you who remain unconvinced, we can survive without being self-aware, most of us do it for years, we can even be happy and successful, but, can we fully experience a true depth of living without it? We all have our favourite ways of doing things and behaving. Knowing what these are and how they impact, both positively and negatively, can give us a huge advantage in life. As we gain self-awareness our experience of life expands, and we stand a better chance of success.

As self-aware people, we know our strengths and weaknesses. We are enthusiastic and positive and take personal responsibility for our actions. We're an inspiration to others. We adapt more easily to change, and we become better people. So why wouldn't we want all that? I'm in! Are you going to come with me on this journey? If you are that's fantastic, read on my friend.

The 'self' is an important concept in self-awareness and shouldn't be underestimated. This is all about knowing ourselves inside and out, warts and all. The more we find out at the start, the easier the journey is going to be.

OK here's a technical bit. The 'Johari window' can be used to help us better understand our relationship with ourselves. Created by Joseph Luft and Harrington Ingham in 1955 it explains the different types of 'self' that we should be aware of when on this journey. Yes, we all have many selves, we're just not aware of them. I'm not going to go through the whole explanation here. There's lots of information out there if you want to know more, but it's worth just giving the definitions of self that underpin the principle.

- **The known self.** This is what we and others see in us. It's visible and open. It's the part of us that we're happy to talk about openly with others. It's easy for us to accept this view of ourselves.
- **The hidden self.** This is what we see in ourselves, but others don't see. In this 'self' we hide things, consciously or sub-consciously.

3

Things that we feel are private about ourselves. We don't want our hidden self to be out in the open in order to protect ourselves. We may be ashamed of what's there and feel vulnerable having our faults and weaknesses exposed. This equally applies to our strengths and talents that we don't want to advertise to the world due to modesty. We all have a hidden self whether we acknowledge it or not.

- **The blind self.** This is what we can't see in ourselves but that others can see in us. We might see ourselves as open-minded when, in reality, others see us as closed off, or vice versa, we might see ourselves as an uptight person while others might consider us open. It's quite common that other people might not be honest. They may not tell us what they see because they don't want to offend us. It's in this area that people sometimes pick up on the fact that what we say and what we do doesn't always match. This can often show up in our body language and betray us. (Non-verbal communication is covered later). This is the self that often trips us up so the more we know ourselves and the less we keep in here, the better.

- **The unknown self.** This is the self that we can't see and neither can others. In here there are likely to be good and bad things. This could be untapped potential, talents, skills, and strengths that have yet to be discovered by us, or other people. This self can slowly reveal itself to us if we allow it to. In other words, if we become more self-aware.

The known self and the hidden self are the two we're most comfortable with just because we can see them; they're open. The blind self and the unknown self are the ones most likely to make us feel uncomfortable. Just knowing that can help. The sides of ourselves we're uncomfortable with are those on which we should focus. The less we keep in there, the better and the more comfortable we will feel about ourselves. The more comfortable we feel, the easier the journey to self-awareness and therefore success.

We now know what self-awareness is. So how can we develop it in ourselves?

Developing self-awareness

Before we can start to make changes in ourselves and become more self-aware we need to understand what it is we're working with, our raw material, if you like. The question to ask is 'Who am I?' This is a process of understanding ourselves that starts with where we currently are. In order to do this, we have to ask ourselves some important questions, and we absolutely have to answer truthfully! We can't lie to ourselves; that would be missing the point of the whole journey.

- Do we have undefined values and beliefs, or lack passion and purpose in our life?
- Are we living a lie, to ourselves and about ourselves?
- Do we react to situations with anger, defensiveness or self-pity?
- Do we feel out of balance in an area of our life either work, family, friends or self?
- Do we over think things, worry and hold grudges?
- Do we react based on what others think or do?

If we can answer 'yes' to any of the above, we need to think about how to change that using some of the tools below. If I'm being honest, I know I can still answer yes to at least three and I've been on this journey a while. To begin with, I could answer yes to all of them so don't worry if that's where you are now. I'll never stop learning all about this and neither should you.

There's a lot we can do to change those 'yes' answers around by applying some basic tools to further our understanding of 'us.'

- **Defining our core values**. These are very personal to us for example 'be there for my children,' 'earn enough to give my family a comfortable life,' 'respect my work colleagues,' 'be honest in all my business dealings.' The list is endless and should reflect the type of person we are or aspire to be. We don't have to actually write a list, although I do. You'll find out later how important lists are to me. We should be 'aware' of them. In the spirit of being open and honest here are some of mine:

- o   Be as open and honest as I can be in all my relationships.
- o   Let go of those negative feelings that don't matter.
- o   Eat healthily and exercise regularly. (Tough one)
- o   Don't take myself too seriously, smile and laugh regularly. (Easy one)
- o   Respect everyone in my relationships.
- o   Do at least one good deed a day.
- o   Find the good in everyone and everything.
- o   Kick my egos butt daily.

You can see that some of these values help me physically and others emotionally but they're all there to help me to succeed and be a better person. They help define me. Some of them are deliberately focused on areas that I know are my weaknesses to enable me to improve. Eventually we don't even have to think about our values they become who we are. Our core values may change over time with our life experiences and challenges we face. It's good to re-evaluate them regularly to make sure they're still relevant.

- **Defining who we want to be in our relationships with others**, 'I want to be a trusted friend,' 'I want to help my friend be a better person,' again the list is personal, and again it doesn't have to be a physical list, just an awareness. We should also think about any boundaries that exist as part of our relationships with others. I've only done this for the key relationships in my life, about ten people. Don't try and boil the ocean here. It's better to have fully defined a few important relationships with people close to you than to have only scratched the surface on lots of less important ones. Those people who are really important in our lives deserve to have us understand exactly what we want out of that relationship even if they don't know it. We don't go around telling everyone what we've defined, but our actions towards them show it, and our relationships are better for it.

- **Staying focused on the present**. That's where life is happening. Life doesn't happen to us in the past or even in the future; it's here and now and we need to run with it and keep up. What's happened in the past is over, done. It can't be undone. If there are lessons we can learn we should do that. Then we need to move on. There's nothing to be gained from dwelling in the past. The future is mostly out of our control. We can try to influence future events, but we'll never have total control of it so it shouldn't take up a disproportionate amount of our time. That leaves us with now! We need to focus on this. This is where we can make a difference to ourselves, our lives and the lives of others, just by being more self-aware and emotionally aware.

- **Acting to put ourselves right**. This is about identifying our weaknesses and potential areas for improvement in our self-awareness. Where we identify something about ourselves that we don't like and where we can act to correct it. For example, I know I can be very defensive when I feel 'wronged' and I can often hold a grudge about it. I struggle to let go of those feelings. When they raise their heads I recognise it and mentally let them go, until the next time! This is the whole point of the journey, to improve our self-awareness and therefore our chance of success.

As I said at the beginning, all the ideas in this book are a complex, interlinked spider's web or network, all influencing and interdependent on each other. I re-assess my own position on a regular basis as I recognise my ability to apply self-awareness slips over time. I'm only human after all, although I suspect there are a lot of people out there who might disagree with that. Actually, even I might disagree sometimes, but I'm sticking to it as my excuse for now.

Awareness of self and emotions can be developed. We can spend some time recognising the areas we need to work on and intentionally making an effort to develop or strengthen those aspects of ourselves. So, how can we become more aware of our strengths and areas for development?

It's important to assess ourselves in order to know what we think our strengths are. We can ask others what they think and be open to hearing the truth. We can complete a formal assessment test. These could include a personality test, discovering our values, our skills, our abilities. There are plenty of these available online. However, they aren't my preferred way of doing this as it's easy to skew the results. In reality, a combination of these is best though I personally only do the tests for a joke.

There are other ways we can assess how self-aware we currently are.

- **Keeping a journal of our feelings.** Writing down what happens, what we're feeling, and how we react. Is there a physical reaction, such as a racing heart? This builds up a picture of our emotions and how we react to them which we can use to improve. Here's an important concept for us to understand. We can't change how we feel, but we can change how we react to that feeling. For example, some situations make me angry. I used to react with negative body language and even aggression, but by recognising that negative response, I can now replace it with a different reaction such as deliberate relaxation or meditation, while I deal with whatever made me angry in the first place. I'm still angry, but I choose to react differently. There are still some people who, because I care deeply, still evoke strong emotional reactions in me, and I recognise that when dealing with those people I need to be consciously self-aware, to ensure I don't overreact. I still do, but then I'm still working on my weaknesses.

- **Making a list of our roles.** We can make a list of our roles in life and write down the feelings connected to each role. We might be a brother, sister, employee, husband, wife, mother, father, list down as many as we can. Our feelings for each role might be happy, frustrated, anxious, again, think of as many as we can. This relates to the previous action of defining who we want to be in our relationships but takes it a step further by defining the feelings associated with it. As before once we've defined those feeling we can address any negative ones.

  An example will probably explain this better. I do some mentoring. If I define my feelings associated with that role some of them would be, fulfilled, satisfied, frustrated, and grateful. When people pick up ideas and run with them, I'm satisfied. When they incorporate that into their lives, I'm fulfilled. When they don't listen or don't understand, I'm frustrated. When they move on as better people I'm grateful that I had the opportunity to make a difference. Get it now?

- **Trying to predict how we will feel.** Trying to predict how we will feel about future events that are likely to happen. If we can do this, then we can start to define and accept the feelings in advance and be proactive about our reactions. We might say "I may feel angry," or "I may feel frustrated." Putting a name to the feeling puts us in control. Think about what would be the right reaction rather than our normal reaction and next time something happens try to react differently. Using the example of mentoring; I can predict that I'll feel frustrated if people appear not to listen. When that happens I prefer to ask them why they don't understand. I'm happy to go over it again rather than throwing my hands up in despair which would have been my previous reaction.

I have said that self-awareness is the beginning of emotional intelligence. Emotionally intelligent people (See later section) plan their days in order to put time aside to build self-awareness. One way to do this is to meditate or reflect daily. This means that we plan to create quiet time for ourselves in the day, away from work or other activities, and spend time focusing on doing something that opens our mind to deeper thoughts. (See section on Spirituality for meditation techniques). I've adjusted this thinking slightly to fit my personal circumstances. My days are usually planned with military precision but, like most plans, proverbial spanners fly in all the time knocking my plans out of touch. If I planned time in for meditation and it then got busted, I'd feel frustrated and stressed. So I don't plan it. Instead, I'm flexible enough to take my opportunities whenever and wherever they arise. I've become very good at quick five minute meditation sessions while in the bathroom. You can laugh if you want to but it's quiet with no distractions and works for me. You just need to find what works for you.

It's important to note that I say we 'develop' awareness and the associated skills. This is not about accumulating information or becoming overly analytical in an academic way. We've been educated at school, but we have no training in being aware of our mind, changing beliefs, emotional reactions, or behaviors. To make these changes requires a different kind of learning and practice.

It's hard to make changes to our emotional reactions and behaviors simply by gaining knowledge and information. If it were that easy, we could all just read a book and instantly change ourselves. Unfortunately, it doesn't work that way. We could read books, and know what we should do but then not actually change anything. In fact, information makes it worse because we end up judging ourselves too harshly when we fail because we expected knowledge alone to do the trick. One of the problems with gaining knowledge is it doesn't require us to take any action. We don't get any new experiences. It's only by experience that we really learn.

This book will tell you all about awareness, but at the end of it you will be no more self-aware than when you started, but you will know what to do to change that, I hope.

Defining values and assumptions

Defining our core values was one of the actions right at the start, remember. You'll see below that one of my core values is not to take myself too seriously. All too often I find myself questioning relationships due to something that was said or done. I over think things and take things to heart. It's an area I constantly try hard to change, letting go of the negative feelings it fosters in me. Strangely enough, letting go of negative feelings is also one of my core values. Values are the principles, standards, morals, ethics, and ideals that guide our lives. Knowing our values is an essential part of building awareness of ourselves. Knowing our values is like following a well-trodden path. We're comfortable and feel secure because we know where we are and where we're heading. We're confident, relaxed, and happy knowing we're on the right path. If we don't know our values, we feel lost and out of control. I hate being out of control so this makes me feel much more comfortable.

Here are my values again and I'll use them as examples in this section.

- Be as open and honest as I can be in all my relationships.
- Let go of those negative feelings that don't matter.
- Eat healthily and exercise regularly. (Tough one)
- Don't take myself too seriously, smile and laugh regularly. (Easy one)

- Respect everyone in my relationships.
- Do at least one good deed a day.
- Find the good in everyone and everything.
- Kick my egos butt daily.

Developing awareness of any assumptions we hold about other people is an important part of emotional intelligence. Self-awareness means that we can't ignore the assumptions we make about ourselves either. I've clearly made some assumptions when defining my values. For a start I've assumed I can identify my negative feelings in order to be able to let them go. I've made that assumption on the basis that I'm already reasonably self-aware, but I'm by no means sure I can identify them all the time, so it's an assumption.

Assumptions about ourselves can be positive or negative. Negative assumptions include thoughts like 'Bad things always happen to me' or 'I don't know how to do this.' Positive assumptions might include thoughts such as 'If I keep trying I will succeed' or 'People are inherently good natured.' I've made that assumption when I say 'I will find the good in everyone.' I truly believe everyone has some good in them, but I'm assuming I'll be able to find it and recognise it. We all subconsciously make these types of assumptions about ourselves, but with self-awareness we acknowledge it openly and seek to improve. Using the personal example above, when I over think things I generate negative assumptions about myself, others, and my relationship with them. I can acknowledge that I do that and try to change those to positive ones. If I assume someone is being mean to me, I look at what was said and try to see it differently. I try to put a positive spin on it and see if maybe I misunderstood. Sometimes I'm right, and sometimes I'm wrong but how I react always changes.

'To have greater self-awareness or understanding means to have a better grasp of reality' —Dalai Lama

To reiterate self-awareness is an essential building block of emotional intelligence. Becoming self -aware is a journey, and we'll probably spend a lifetime learning about ourselves. As we improve our self-awareness we also improve our experience of life, create opportunities for a better work-life balance, become aware of our emotions, and improve our ability to respond to change. As a result, our lives and relationships improve as we go so even though we may never reach the end we reap the benefits as we go along.

Positive steps to improve our self-awareness

OK, so we've covered the basic building blocks of self-swareness, values, roles, assumptions, and skills. So how do we improve from here? What are the next steps?

There are some things we can do to help with our journey to improve self-awareness and also to make it easier. One thing to note, as I said before, developing self-awareness does *not* happen through reading books, including this one, we need to get out there, do these things and experience the results.

- **Listening to ourselves**. The first step is to assess what we're really saying, in other words, to listen to ourselves. What's our mind telling us? Are our thoughts negative and therefore making us feel bad? Or is our mind in a glass half full mode and looking on the bright side? To help in doing this, we can sit quietly and listen to what we're thinking. Make sure our surroundings are quiet and right for concentration. If it's too hard to concentrate, then standing in front of a mirror and describing to ourselves how we look and listening to what we're saying helps. Are the things we say to ourselves, about ourselves, positive or negative? Are we saying 'I love my hair like this.' Or 'My hair looks a mess.' If our thoughts are consistently negative, that's a sign we should re-evaluate how we think.

- **Using all our senses**. Our senses, mainly sight and hearing, provide us with a lot of insight into the world we interact with, ourselves, other people and the situations we find ourselves in. One thing we need to be aware of is that these senses are often skewed by our own assumptions and ideas. If we have negative opinions on something and we see or hear it then we bias our senses with that negativity. In other words, we can't always trust what they tell us. If I believe I've got wrinkles, I'll probably see wrinkles in the mirror. OK, I do see wrinkles in the mirror.

  The next time someone, or we feel that someone, judges us or has made us feel bad about ourselves we can take a step back and look at why we think and feel like that. Could we have interpreted it differently? Could we have been mistaken about the intention? Quite often we'll find that our interpretation was clouded by our own negative ideas and assumptions. If we don't like someone then even if they say something nice we will often hear it as negative. Guilty!

- **Letting our feelings and emotions out**. This is not always easy, and I find this particularly difficult to do. It can be very hard if we're not the sort of person who likes to look too closely at how we feel and why but, trust me, it's worth doing. Our feelings are a spontaneous and emotional response to the events we experience. Unlike our senses, they give us genuine and true information about what's happening around us and to us. If we can recognise them and let those feelings out, we'll understand them better. In other words, be more self-aware. There's a section on expressing emotion later in the book.

Advancing our self-awareness.

If we're really into this journey, then there are more advanced actions we can take to increase our understanding of self-awareness. Read them and see how you feel. If we've followed everything so far and, more importantly, put it into practice, then we're already somewhat self-aware. Now we can dig deeper into it and see what we can really find out about ourselves. A lot of the following leads into the later section about emotion as part of self-awareness.

Remember when the chips are down we're stuck with ourselves for the rest of our lives, so we might as well get to know, understand, and actually like who we truly are. So here are some more advanced self-awareness techniques. As you'll see, the web-like nature of this means most of these will crop up later on.

- **Understanding our emotions.** Our emotions drive our lives. They determine the mood we're in and therefore the sort of day we're having. They also set the tone for all our relationships. As emotions are such a powerful force in our lives, we need to try to understand them. We also need to learn to be aware of them and their positive and negative impacts on us. We need to realise that we can't change them, we can only change our reaction to them. Love and passion are two of the most powerful positive emotions we can experience and can lead to great achievements. We should strive never to repress our emotions even when society tells us we should. A later section in the book deals with emotions in more detail.

- **Being grateful for everything we have.** Gratitude is something that people who are self-aware don't take for granted. It's so simple, being grateful each day for the good things in our lives makes us feel better, costs nothing and makes us see the world in a different light. Why wouldn't we be grateful for that? It can also help us to become aware of our values, our beliefs, our emotions and brings with it the recognition that we can make a difference in the world. Gratitude is also covered under emotions.

- **Using our willpower.** This is not one of my strengths but we all have willpower, to a greater or lesser extent, and being self-aware can help us to use it to the best advantage. Self-awareness allows us to make conscious decisions regarding the use of willpower and willpower itself can prevent us from straying from the path of awareness. If we're aware of how our willpower works best for us, then we can use it to our advantage. I've tried to use willpower to exercise more with mixed results, but at least I do more than I used to do so I guess it's a small win for me. I use my will power with a little more success keeping my ego in check, but it doesn't always work. I need to try harder with this one.

- **Focusing our attention.** Discovering where to focus our attention gives us freedom to use any time gained productively. If we focus on the priorities, then we get more done in less time. As we've seen before we can't change our emotions but we can choose to re-focus our attention somewhere else. If we can direct our attention elsewhere then learning to direct our lives becomes easier. There's a section later that deals with focus and concentration and this also leads into time management. There's that spider's web of interlinked ideas again!

- **Learning to accept things.** We all need to be able to accept those things which we can't change. This means we need to learn to be aware when something can't be changed. Perhaps the biggest category here is the external impacts on us. That would be events that are out of our control. If we can accept them, then we can learn to react positively to them even if they're bad. The same principle applies to our emotions. Personally, I'm pretty good at this although it takes me longer than it should. I'm still learning!

- **Self-observation.** In our own minds we play different roles in different situations in our lives. Sometimes we'll be strong other times acquiescent, and each character we play is like a different personality. You won't believe how many personalities I manifest. If I ever need counseling, I'm in trouble. These personalities have different impacts on our emotions both good and bad. This is quite an advanced self-awareness trait but if we can recognise which character is being played at any one time, and we understand the impact that character has on the way we behave, then we can control all the negative impacts of the emotions that are in play even though we can't control the emotions themselves. I'd advise reading that several times to get your head round it.

- **Noticing what we say.** This links to the earlier step of listening to ourselves. Sometimes what we say comes with an emotional price. We should be aware of any strong opinions we have and especially what we say to others when voicing those opinions. If we're aware not only of what we say but the potential impact of it on others, we can reduce conflict in our lives and gain more respect from others. The words we use represent our core values, which underpin them, often without our knowledge. If we're unaware of the values being implied by our words, we can't control the impact of them on us or others, and life becomes a bit more complicated. This reinforces the importance of defining our values right up front.

- **Learning to live for ourselves.** We often don't behave the way we want to out of fear. Fear of someone else's reaction to what we do. We also change our behaviour because we don't want someone else to react badly. This means we're living our lives based on our reactions to the outside influence of others. That's not living our own lives, and once we recognise that, we can start to change it. Understanding and being aware of why we do this, and the emotions that underpin it, allows us to change the way we behave and be more open with ourselves. It allows us to be more proactive and less reactive.

- **Forgiveness.** This is powerful, and it's probably the most generous thing we can do in our lives, and because of that, it has its own section later. It allows us to let go of regrets, judgments, resentment, and anger. All those negative emotions disappear if we have the awareness to forgive others and most importantly ourselves. There are no excuses for not being able to forgive when we recognise the benefits of doing so. It makes us feel better. Sometimes it can be hard to forgive, and it can take willpower to do it. I personally understand that and try to always put this into practice. Sometimes it can take me longer than others particularly if it means letting go of some strong emotional reactions, but I get there in the end.

- **Learning to have a quiet mind.** We all have times when our minds just will not shut up! We can't stop the thoughts jumping around all over the place. We become tense and stressed. It's not easy to quiet our minds and feel at peace. We can try to deal with each thing in turn and answer any questions but usually there's too much going on in there to know where to begin. It's a catch twenty two. In order to address the issues running around we need to be able to think clearly, but we can't think clearly because of all the noise in our heads. The only answer I've found to this is to meditate in order to initially clear my mind. Once my mind is clearer I can start to introduce each thought one by one, and deal with them as honestly and with as much self-awareness as possible. If at any time my mind starts racing off again, I go back to the meditation. Rinse and repeat as required.

How good are we at being self-aware?

Here's a bit of fun to see how far we've come so far.

Imagine we're sitting in front of another person. We have to tell that person all about ourselves, but we can't mention any outside influences. No talking about what happens in our lives, or our friends, or our family. We can only talk about ourselves in terms of our behaviour, strengths and weaknesses, feelings and emotions, only the internal influences. This uses all our self-awareness to get across who we are in a meaningful way. What would we say?

OK, I'll go first, this is me describing me!

I'm a natural introvert who expends a lot of willpower trying to be an extrovert, with mixed success. I'm naturally emotional but, because I'm aware of that, I try to express my emotions in a positive way. Most of the time I struggle to keep my ego at bay. I'm very good with positive emotions such as love, passion, gratitude, and forgiveness as well as showing compassion. I'm an empath. I have a wicked, but weird, sense of humour. I'm an optimist, and my glass is definitely half full. I'm naturally disorganised, but I've learned to live with it by becoming a 'control freak!' My time management is good but has to be constantly watched, and I embrace emotional intelligence.

Wow, that really is me, and now you know who I am. So who are you? Try it, dig deep into your self-awareness and describe who you are.

The way we perceive ourselves is important for understanding our feelings, emotions and our reaction to them. It's easy to get carried away with all the noise in our heads and the effect it has on us. We can all cope with life so long as it's going smoothly but what happens when there's change or upheaval? This is when self-awareness really comes into play, allowing us to interpret and challenge what we're thinking and feeling, alter the way we react to our emotions, and change the way we behave. This reduces the negative impact on our lives. This is particularly true and even more important when the change and emotions are to do with relationships. Self-awareness can open up a whole raft of possibilities for us.

Self-awareness and change

Self-awareness involves change. There's no getting away from it. If we want to be self-aware we need to change how we see and react to everything. It's all about challenging the way we see and react to ourselves. If we really don't like change in our lives we need to take this section to heart and try to understand why we don't like it and then do something about it. Change it!

Embracing change involves going on a journey with our emotions. This journey has a path and involves feelings of denial, resistance, desperation, exploration and then finally commitment. For each of these, there are coping mechanisms we can use. Being self-aware ensures we're able to comfortably and successfully cope with change. In other words, we can be resilient. Below I've listed the stages of coping with change and the ways we can manage them.

At first, we're in denial. We avoid the topic, whatever it is, and we appear unconcerned. We can end up lying to ourselves, and we refuse to take the initiative, preferring to sit back and wait for others to act. We carry on as if nothing is happening, in other words, head in the sand, ostrich mentality. At this stage, we need people to help us see and accept the change and make the reality visible to us. We need to discuss what the change means to stop ourselves from getting stuck here.

Next, we show resistance. We sometimes show anger, complain and blame others or conversely, we become passive and exhausted, possibly overwhelmed. We can become preoccupied with the change and can't think beyond it. It can take up all our time. In order to get over this stage, we need to communicate our concerns to people who will listen and try to focus on what we can control.

Then, we move into desperation. We try to walk away, or we may even try to fight it. We withdraw and lose hope. At this time, we need to find people to support us and encourage us to move forward. We don't want to get stuck on this step.

Then, we start to move forward into exploration. This is the real turning point. We ask questions and seek alternatives, and we look at future possibilities. We may even take risks and generate ideas for the future. It's good if we have patient people to lead us at this point and to facilitate the positive points keeping us on the right path.

Finally, we get to commitment. We feel in control and stable. We can reflect on what we've learned, and we start looking forward to the future. It's good to have someone to celebrate with now and to unite in a community around the new normal. We've embraced and accepted the change and move on with our lives.

As we can see this journey is not really a one-off exercise, we need to repeat it as often as we feel it's needed to keep moving forward. I'm lucky, my work is all about change, so I rarely have to go through this cycle. I tend to go straight to exploration and commitment, but I'm very aware that others do have to go through the whole cycle and I'm also aware enough to know how to support them. The steps on this journey aren't necessarily discreet, they often overlap with each other.

Dedication to self-awareness

We now know what self-awareness is and how it can help us. We've defined our values, looked at our assumptions and roles. We've even moved on and looked at some more advanced 'stuff' on self-awareness. We've checked our progress, and we understand the changes we can make to ourselves and how change impacts us. It's starting to look like self-awareness needs some dedication from us in order to make any further difference in our lives.

To really embrace self-awareness and move ourselves forward it's going to take a bit more focus. In order to change our minds and behaviours. We have to put in some effort. We get comfortable doing the same things and reacting in the same ways that it becomes habit forming because it takes less effort on our part. Doing things the same way is a dangerous habit as we're often doing the wrong thing time and again. If we're not aware of this, then we have no commitment to put it right. Very few people champion the cause of self-awareness, and it often goes against many of the societal values we're taught. A good example is admitting we're wrong. Self-awareness advocates that we should admit when we're wrong and learn from it but society often heaps scorn or criticism on us for doing just that. We can often find ourselves isolated in our opinions.

Often it's easier and less painful to go with the status quo and not embrace our own personal improvement. It's easier just to listen to other people when they tell us that's how life is but if we do that we'll never improve or grow and never fully understand ourselves. As a result, we'll never reach our full potential or achieve the success we want. That's quite a hard message to live with, but we've come so far we can't give up now.

It's hard to go against the norm. To question every opinion put before us. Our own brains will try to oppose us as it's not the comfortable option. We only need to look back at some of the advanced topics listed earlier to see just what can be involved in pursuing this path. This is what I mean by needing some dedication to move forward.

The benefits of being self-aware.

Have I put you off yet? I hope not. In case you're feeling rattled and unsure about doing this I'm going to go through the benefits, to get you back on track, and give you some motivation to continue.

We've established that self-awareness entails being conscious of who we are and how we think in order for us to better understand ourselves and facilitate positive change in our lives. Teaching people to become self-aware is now used as part of Cognitive Behavioural Therapy or CBT, in helping people overcome their anxiety and fears, to help them to own their thoughts and feelings in order to change. The benefits are beginning to be acknowledged and are starting to be more widely used.

The benefits of self-awareness are too numerous to list them all here. We can gain control of our lives and behaviour and be more flexible and confident. We can deal with challenges head on and in the right way. We can interact and communicate with others better. Make better decisions, reduce our stress levels and as a result put more into life and get more out of life. We can succeed.

If we have an understanding of how we naturally prefer to behave, we'll not only be more efficient, but we'll form more successful relationships. This is because we'll be in a position to understand what works for us in a given situation, and we'll be able to adapt ourselves and act differently if our usual style isn't working for us. We'll be able to identify our weaknesses and put them right, set personal objectives for ourselves in order to improve those weaknesses and inspire others to do the same. We can focus on what motivates us, in order to develop our potential, and find new ways to tackle challenges. We'll avoid feelings of frustration when others don't do things the way we do. All of this adds to our feelings of well-being and adds real value to our lives and those of others.

In order to reap a lot of the benefits of self-awareness, we need to be able to work at our full potential. We need to know and appreciate the learning, personality and management styles that are instinctive to us. Imagine how much more effective we'll be if we understand why we do things in a particular way and why we're naturally good at certain things, yet struggle with others. Why we look forward to doing one thing but hate, or even actively avoid, doing another. Why we react to different situations or events in the way we do. Why we get on better with some people more than others. Why we feel motivated or demotivated in a given situation. We'll also understand the influences behind these feelings and what drives them.

In order to benefit from self-awareness, we need to understand ourselves, obviously. Part of understanding how to work on being self-aware is knowing our own personality. This relates to our character and behaviour and is what makes us react to external and internal events in certain ways.

There are five common personality types, usually applied to how we work, but equally applicable to our personal lives. As we read the descriptions, we can see how each one will use the knowledge that self-awareness brings in a different way. There's no right or wrong way on the path to self-awareness only what works for each of us.

- **The realist:** This is a loyal and steady person who meets deadlines, does what they say they will and believes in established rules.
- **The idealist:** This type of person uses their own inner values to make sense of events in life and focuses on personal growth and the growth of others.
- **The innovator:** This person is energetic and creative, takes inspiration from various sources, enjoys a flexible environment with few rules but allows opportunities for fun.
- **The leader:** These are natural managers, who strive for efficiency, see the bigger picture and make clear plans for the future.

- **The strategist:** This type is intellectually curious, uses objective thinking and forward planning to find original solutions to problems.

In reality, we will all show traits from all five personality types, but one personality style will almost always be dominant. With me, I do what I say I will do and focus on growth but I'm also creative and a natural planner. My dominant style is 'Innovator.' Probably because of the lack of rules and the potential for having some fun.

The various personality styles all show themselves in the way we communicate. This not only refers to what we say but how we say it. Our choice of words, tone, and communication can make all the difference. For example, do we prefer to communicate by email, allowing us to choose what's discussed and control the words, or do we prefer to meet face to face with people and ask them questions, and then listen carefully to everything that has been said and have a discussion with them? We should consider what it's like to be on the receiving end of our message, whatever it is and however it's delivered. From this perspective, we'll be in a position to make sure it's understood and gets the desired response. There's a more detailed section on communication later on.

Now we're aware of what's involved on the journey to self-awareness, the steps we have to take, the path to follow, and the potential ups and downs. It's your choice to carry on but be aware this journey never ends; it's a circular path, a lifetime of constant 'tweaking' of ourselves to stay on it. The benefits, for me, outweigh all that. I believe I'm a better person and more successful as a result of self-awareness, but I can't say I'm fully self-aware and I never will be able to. That's not a negative thought but me being honest about what this entails.

Summary of actions from this section:

- Define our core values, relationships and roles.
- Journal our feelings.
- Identify our weaknesses and act to put them right.
- Define the assumptions we make
- Listen to and understand ourselves

- Forgive, let go and be grateful.
- Understand and learn to accept change.

Ego

'Negative states of mind, such as anger, resentment, fear, envy, and jealousy, are products of the ego.' —Eckhart Tolle

Being self-aware means understanding the impact our ego has on the way we behave and treat others. I used to think of the ego as just a passive manifestation of myself. I never gave it too much thought, to be honest. I was so wrong. Now that I understand the implications of that belief, I can work to repair the damage on myself and my relationships.

Ego is something we should really try to get rid of from our lives or minimize as much as possible. Ego is a negative force. It's totally dependent on outside influences, things out of our control, and it's limiting to us and those around us. We need to let go of the concept of always having to be right; it's OK to say we 'don't know' or to admit we're wrong even though that may go against all we've been taught. If we admit when we're wrong or when we've made a mistake, other people will actually begin to trust us. They'll recognise that we're being honest and that we have integrity. This concept can be hard to take on board particularly in a world, or environment, where failure is considered a bad thing. Failure is not a bad thing unless we don't learn from it. That's the key message here; we have to learn from our mistakes.

As a self-aware person, we should be able to identify when ego intrudes on our lives. Personally, the biggest example for me is when I feel I've been treated unfairly, then my ego rears its ugly head, and I behave completely out of character. I become selfish, jealous, and downright nasty sometimes. I really need to work on that one, but at least I'm aware of it. Most of the time I'm able to look at what happened and understand what I can control and what I can't control and then I can start to let it go. I'm truly sorry to anyone who's been on the receiving end of my ego. It couldn't have been pleasant for you. Forgive me? Please.

Ego comes from fear, fear of judgment and fear of failure. Fear is 'False Evidence Appearing Real.' Getting rid of ego means not taking things personally. Ego relies on our perception of others and their perceptions of us, and it leads to a blame culture. If we aren't afraid, or we can recognise that the impact of our fear of something can be removed, then we don't need ego. Ego sits on our shoulder like our proverbial inner devil, all we need to do is empower our inner angel, self-awareness, to overcome it. Sounds easy, doesn't it? Sometimes it is, but more often it's not.

I've experienced a bad case of ego, as a result of fear, while writing this book. Fear of failure and judgment and fear of being ridiculed. I've never done anything like this before, and because I'm putting so much of myself into it, it's become very important to me. I'm emotionally invested in it. My inner devil was in the ascendant. If this book is ever published, and if you're reading this I can assume it is, then I've successfully conquered my ego in this particular instance and my self-aware angel has won the battle. Yes! However, at the time of writing, that is by no means a done deal!

We should seek to understand when we feel unsatisfied, unfulfilled or incomplete as these easily lead to the emergence of our 'old friend' ego. What are the triggers for these negative feelings? How can we feel the way we want to feel? Think about it!

The answer, of course, is to change and improve our self-awareness. We can't stop the triggers as they're external and aren't under our control. What we can do is learn to find out what it is we want by analysing our actions and reactions rather than the outcomes of them. The outcomes are external forces on us, but our actions and reactions are under our control.

We can challenge ourselves and ask searching questions about our actions. Once we're aware of and can understand our actions, we can control them, and then we can change them for the better. Using my example, I can't stop myself from sometimes feeling I've been unfairly treated, but I know it's a trigger for my ego. I don't want to react with anger and selfishness, so I've looked long and hard at how I can turn that reaction around. I've learned that if I stop myself from giving a knee jerk reaction and take the time to think about what was said or done, I feel calmer and more able to give a measured response. Often I can actually see that my initial reaction is wrong and that I misunderstood. As a result, I feel better, and I don't make matters worse by overreacting.

I don't know anyone who's managed to rid themselves of ego in its entirety, but I do know some who are close. Personally, I'm still working on this one. I have occasional small wins, but when I go to congratulate myself, I realise that's my ego kicking in and pride taking over. I can't win, but I'll keep trying, and I'm hoping to make myself a better, nicer person one step at a time. Each time I do manage to overcome my ego is a step in the right direction.

Relationships

'The meeting of two personalities is like the contact of two chemical substances: if there is any reaction both are transformed.' —Carl Jung

Good relationships are precious. It makes sense to use our own precious time and energy to foster and care for them. Whether it's family, friends, work colleagues or even casual acquaintances, we all form temporary and/or permanent relationships with others throughout our lives. Self-awareness plays a key role in all these relationships. We need to be able to have good quality, authentic communication with all these people. We also need to know what role we play and where the boundaries are in each relationship. If we cross a hard boundary, then the relationship could be in jeopardy. Above all, if a relationship is going to be of benefit to both parties, then we need to be presenting the real us, not what we think someone wants to see or what we think we should be, but the real, honest us. This is why being truthful about the roles we play is so important. This was covered at the start of self-awareness. To do this, we need to be aware of who we are in the relationship, friend, lover, parent, or teacher? The real us will be and behave very differently depending on who we are, what role we play, and what the boundaries are. It's possible, even common, to be multiple things to one relationship. Relationships aren't always simple. Some of the most complex relationships can be the most fulfilling. Someone actually quoted me on that once. He knows who he is.

Let's look at an example of a partner or lover. In the beginning, the relationship is going really well, but even so, we're human and so a part of us will worry about the potential for it to fall apart or go wrong in some way. Consciously, or subconsciously, we'll analyse and try to understand how we would feel if that were to happen and we'll almost certainly come to the conclusion that we'll feel sad, unloved or a whole lot of other negative emotions. If we don't like that answer, in other words, we recognise we'll feel bad; we'll start to put strategies in place to minimize the impact on our emotions. This is human nature; it's self-preservation. One possible strategy is to decide to back off from the relationship, to cool it down and not get too heavily involved. If we do this, it'll mean we don't allow ourselves to benefit fully from a potentially fulfilling relationship and that would be a real shame. There is an alternative. If we're self-aware, we can try this instead. Rather than backing away we can communicate, tell our partner our fears and concerns and share them with them. More importantly, we can share how they make us feel. Let them know we're insecure and scared and why. Maybe they'll admit to having similar fears and feeling the same emotions as we are. We can then agree to be open and honest, and communicate, how we feel at all times, letting each other know any negative feelings as soon as they arise. If we're self-aware, then we can act to change any negative impacts and improve our feelings and emotions and also those of our partner. As a result, the relationship stands a better chance of flourishing, and we can hope for a better outcome. Doesn't that scenario feel better? By applying self-awareness, we've changed what could have been a wasted opportunity into a chance for a better future and a successful relationship.

It's only natural to want to protect ourselves from getting hurt in a relationship. We're human after all. This is particularly true when we're in a romantic or intimate relationship where our hearts are deeply involved. It's human nature to want to protect our hearts. We create plans and strategies, even if only subconsciously, to help us survive that potential hurt. Often the other person in the relationship has no idea these strategies even exist. We are in control of, and responsible for, not only our own awareness but in this case the awareness of others as well. We can choose to be open with others about the ways we protect ourselves and just maybe the need for that protection will go away.

If we're self-aware then communication, within a relationship, becomes easier and more open. We understand why we act and react in the way we do and that understanding reduces our stress and allows us to be more even tempered and less confrontational. We take responsibility for our actions rather than seeking to blame. Self-awareness reduces conflict and increases empathy, leading to compromise and compromise is good for the success of all relationships.

Building better relationships entails making an effort to connect with others, even when we don't want to. Getting out there and accepting people for who and what they are, nurturing our friendships and being open to making new ones.

We've seen the benefits of self-awareness to ourselves, so it goes without saying that it's also beneficial in our relationships with others. Relationships are easy until there's emotional upheaval. This is the same whether we're at work or in our personal life. When we can change the way our mind views the upheaval and our emotional reaction, then we can change our reaction to those emotions. Then we can go on to change the emotional quality of our relationships for the better and open up entirely new opportunities in our lives.

Having a clear understanding, or being self-aware, of our thoughts and behaviour patterns helps us to understand other people. This ability to empathise facilitates better personal and professional relationships.

Empathy in relationships

This is important so if, while you've been reading this, you're starting to flag, go and put on some coffee or make a cup of tea and come back ready to focus.

Empathy is our ability to relate to others emotions, thoughts, and experiences. It's much deeper than sympathy. It's about truly understanding someone else's situation from their perspective, placing ourselves in their shoes and feeling what they are feeling. Empathy helps resolve conflict and is an important life skill. It enables us to give people the support they need and help them deal with challenges they may be facing. The better people know and understand each other the better they interact.

People who are empathic share a number of characteristics. These can be developed over time as part of our self-awareness journey. An empathic person is an active listener, totally focused on the person they're talking to. They can interpret body language and non-verbal signals well and have a high degree of emotional intelligence (EQ is covered later). They ask probing, in-depth questions in order to get a better understanding of the other person. They are personally self-aware and acknowledge their own emotions and how they can impact and affect others. They are curious and take a genuine interest in others and also embrace diversity, being completely non-judgemental, and instead they accept and embrace potential differences.

Most of us have a certain level of empathy already, but we can work to become even more empathic. I've concentrated on this area and consider myself to be highly empathic. As a result, I find I can make a positive difference in my relationships. There are four simple ways we can increase our ability to be empathic.

- **We can engage with people who are different from us at every opportunity**. This could be as simple as spending time with another social group or talking to someone we normally never would. We all have different ways of doing things, relating to others, and making decisions. It's much easier to empathise with someone who thinks and acts in a similar way to us. It's much harder, however, to empathise with those who behave and believe differently. Engaging with people who are different from us opens us up to alternative feelings and emotions giving us the opportunity to look at things from a different perspective, one which we haven't ourselves experienced. This helps us to grow as a person.

- **We can create personal connections with people by asking questions**. We can show an interest in the people we meet, whether at work or socially. Ask them about themselves, their hobbies and interests, their families and their aspirations. It's important that we remember what they've said so we can use this to help us with conversations next time we meet. This means applying active listening techniques which are covered below. The more we know about someone, the better we can understand what makes them tick. This allows us to better put ourselves in their shoes and show a greater level of empathy.

- **We can be active listeners.** We shouldn't interrupt when listening to others, for a start, it's just plain rude. We should check our understanding of what's being said regularly by asking for clarification and asking questions when we don't understand fully. This builds on what the other person has said and in summarising, or paraphrasing them, deepens our understanding of the conversation. It's only polite to give people our full attention and stay focused. It stands to reason we should never check social media or our email, or even look at the time while listening. It's a big 'no no' but have a look at friends and colleagues and see how often it happens. It's scary.

- **One of the easiest ways to be more empathic is to learn to interpret body language or non-verbal communication signals.** This can tell us a lot about the person we're communicating with. We can familiarise ourselves with basic signals such as tone of voice, posture, gestures, and eye contact and look out for them in our interactions. This can take practice so we can try it out when we're with friends. Trying not to focus solely on the words they're saying but instead paying attention to their body language and how they say things. This can give us a deeper understanding of the message they're trying to get across. As an example, we all know that if someone is standing with their arms folded across their chest, they're feeling defensive, possibly angry and maybe even afraid. If we look for other signals, we can understand which of these emotions is being experienced and ensure our own actions and reactions are appropriate. If we react as though we think they're angry when they're really feeling afraid, then we risk making their fear worse. That's why it's so important to apply some empathy.

Developing empathy takes a certain degree of effort and focus. It's not always easy to understand why people think or feel the way they do or to be able to recognise it. However, people who take the time to empathise with others can reap the real rewards that these deeper relationships bring. If you know someone who's an empath, you'll know how easy is it to relate to them, talk to them, and be with them.

Having a clear understanding of our thought and behaviour patterns helps us to understand other people. This ability to empathise facilitates better relationships which adds enormous value to our own lives and is a key deliverable in our success. The benefits of showing empathy, even a little bit, are enormously rewarding.

Stress management

'If you ask what is the single most important key to longevity, I would have to say it is avoiding worry, stress and tension. And if you didn't ask me, I'd still have to say it.' —*George Burns*

Let me start by saying not all stress is bad. Good stress can drive us forward to help us achieve success and even greatness if we recognise it and work with it. So what is good stress? It could be excitement, when our hearts beat faster, and hormones rush around our system. The sort of stress we experience on a roller coaster or at the start of a new relationship is considered good stress. This good stress helps us feel alive and motivates us. If you doubt that, then ask an adrenaline junkie. If we're able to recognise the activities and triggers for good stress, we can actively make sure we repeat them and so enrich our lives. The key is to find a balance between having enough good stress to improve our performance but not so much that there's a negative impact on our health. Stress management is the ability to recognise the different types and sources of stress and, not surprisingly, to manage them.

Studies have identified typical stressful situations in our lives. These include family problems, mental illness, elderly and child care, financial problems, legal issues, grief and loss, work-life imbalance, health problems, lack of good time management, and change that is imposed upon us. If we're self-aware and we know that one, or many, of these situations apply to us, we can cope better to reduce our stress levels.

Stress is only bad when we can't cope with the effects of it and it becomes too much. It's possible to turn some bad stress into good stress if we train ourselves to respond in a positive way to the triggers. We need to be self-aware enough to recognise those triggers in the first place. I used to get stressed when faced with presenting in front of a large audience, but I can now recognise that the trigger for that stress was fear. What if I forget what I'm talking about? What if they don't like or agree with me? Of course, I now realise it doesn't matter. If I forget things I'll just admit it, check my notes and laugh with the audience. I don't really mind if they like me or not as I probably won't see any of them ever again. By recognising my triggers I've negated them. Those triggers can't impact me anymore, and I no longer feel stress. Are you starting to understand the circular nature of all this yet? Look at the situation as a challenge to be overcome; it's all about our perception. There are tools and techniques we can use to control bad stress, but they're different depending on our own situations.

- **Avoid stimulants**. Reduce our intake of caffeine, nicotine, and alcohol. Get the picture? I'm not avoiding caffeine even if I know I should.
- **Exercise regularly**. This is a big one for me. I'm not naturally a sporty person (apart from swimming) and this one takes effort and persistence on my part. But it's worth it, even twenty minutes five times a week. I'm so bad at this I even bought a treadmill because I'm too lazy to go to a gym. I'm lucky; I have people in my life

who nag me. I've actually asked them to make sure I do my twenty minutes, and I am grateful for them as they keep me honest.

- **Get enough sleep.** This is a tough one as it's different for each of us. I can survive happily on five hours a night, but I know people who struggle if they get less than seven or eight. We have to listen to our bodies and go with what they tell us. Trust me; you don't want to know me if I have less than five hours and I admit to having to resort to caffeine to keep going if I don't get it. As a result, of course, my stress levels increase and I become even worse. I'm not sure if I'll ever really learn to break that cycle.

- **Learn to relax.** I mean really relax, not using our brains type of relaxing. Meditation is ideal, and it's worth perfecting it to find what works for you. I cover basic meditation later. If you can't switch off your brain completely, then go for a walk or read, watch TV or a movie, anything to distract your brain from stress temporarily. This won't fix the problem, but it will give your brain some relief.

- **Get into the habit of talking.** Good open and honest conversation about how we feel, not just a chat. We mustn't lie to ourselves or others about why we are feeling stressed. We need to get it out of our system and then let it go. I find that writing all my negative reactions in an email, (or a letter if technology isn't your thing) helps but please don't put anyone in the 'to' field just in case! We've all heard the stories! Leave it for a while then go back and reread it as many times as it takes, edit it if you want and then when you feel better about it, delete it or tear it up. Then let it go.

- **Be aware.** Not only of the actual stress you're feeling but what triggers it and what works, for you, to control it. Investigate how you can turn the bad stress into good stress. If you can be aware of this and change it, then it becomes easier to manage.

- **Take control.** Oh how I love that word! Being in control reduces the likelihood of becoming stressed; it puts us in our comfort zone. Feeling out of control is a big trigger for me. I've been called a control freak so many times that I believe it's true; I am one! If I start to feel stressed and I can take control and deal with it, then I do, immediately! No procrastination! If there's nothing I can do, then I let it go and avoid the stress. This is easier said than done and takes practice. At first it can be a bit like herding cats when our minds go off in all directions looking for an answer, but even cats can be brought under control eventually. Actually probably not but hey! This is a trick I have pretty much perfected, but even this control freak has relapses.

- **Learn time management.** There's a whole section on this later on. Once you learn to manage your time effectively the stress associated with your email backlog, tasks piling up, deadlines being missed and generally being overwhelmed with everything on your to-do list goes away. Again it's all about control. Are you seeing a pattern or recurring theme?
- **Learn to say no.** This is a big one for a lot of people, including me. It's tough to say no for fear of being rude or impolite, letting someone down or having someone think badly of us, (there's ego rearing its head, again) but, it's our life and our choice to say no, and we shouldn't have to justify it to anyone. There's more information on this later under work-life balance. Now you can start to see the nature of the information here as a spider's web.

Stress can manifest in a variety of ways, and part of being self-aware is learning to recognise and manage them. If you suffer from any of the symptoms below, then you could be under stress.

Headache, nausea, sleep disturbance, shaking, pain, tension, irritability, depression, restlessness, anxiety, reduced self-esteem, tunnel vision, eating problems, lack of concentration, aggression, negativity, carelessness, withdrawal.

Ways of coping with stress are personal to us, but a regular routine for eating and sleeping is a good place to start along with learning to relax or meditate. We can conquer most of the bad stress in our lives with a little bit of application and perseverance. The benefits to our health are enormous.

I would never presume to say I don't get stressed, we all do. I've learned to manage it and therefore cope with it by using self-awareness. I've become a much more laid back person as a result. Sometimes maybe a bit too laid back.

Motivation

*'Success is not final, failure is not fatal: it is the courage
to continue that counts.'* —*Winston Churchill*

What makes us get out of bed in the morning? Why do we do certain things even when we don't enjoy them? Some people will go the extra mile while others are reluctant to do so, why? We do it because it satisfies a need in us, but we also need to be aware that these needs change over time. Motivation is the driver behind satisfying these needs. Once our basic needs are satisfied, food, water, and shelter, then personal needs come into play, emotional well-being, enjoyment, and fulfillment. If the effort we put into something is balanced by the reward we get out of it, then we'll feel motivated.

Just as it's important to understand our values, it's also important to understand what underpins them. What motivates us to have those values and live by them? We can take responsibility for our own motivation, but we all need a little positive reinforcement from our motivational muse now and then, particularly when we find ourselves in a negative funk. If we don't know what motivates us, then how can we pull ourselves out? Quite often our values and purpose are motivation enough in their own right. If one of our values is to be there for our kids, then there's our motivation, right there. Sometimes we need a little extra inspiration to keep on track.

It's important to identify the things which really keep us engaged and on task and also the things which boost our morale. Maintaining our motivation is a long term thing. Quick solutions don't last.

How can we improve our motivation?

In order to play an active role in our own lives and our own personal development, it's important to identify and understand the things that make us feel engaged, the things which help us to keep our morale high. There are three steps we can take to do this.

- **Identify and understand what satisfies us.** We can think about the things that we've done or seen in our lives that have given us a sense of satisfaction. We can then identify what it was or is about them that made us feel that way. We can actually do the same with the things that we haven't enjoyed or that haven't satisfied us, so we have a full picture of not only motivators but de-motivators as well. For me, it's the ability to create things. I love the feeling when a painting or drawing comes together into something that inspires people or makes them feel good. I can capture that feeling and apply it to other things I do. It's a need to make people feel good. As a result, I try to do that even at work. When I succeed, then I feel motivated to carry on.
- **Focus on the present.** We can look at the things we identified above that satisfy us and apply them to our current circumstances. Think about how we would include more of the things that we enjoy and minimize the things that we don't. It's important to give the here and now a positive balance.
- **Act to change things.** We can weigh up the benefits of any potential changes and decide whether they're worth the effort in order to achieve our goals. If they are then, we can change them.

On the flip side of motivation is obviously de-motivation. There are signs to warn us if we or someone else is de-motivated. We become unclear about our goals and objectives and feel confused about our path in life. We feel out of control (that scares me!). We are dismissive of others' advice and feelings, and we become self-centered. We tend to need more direction and supervision and lack the ability to motivate ourselves or even think for ourselves. We can be moody, which has a negative impact on those we live and work with. Eventually, this will drive people away. Let's look at an example of a de-motivating event and what we can do to improve it.

Imagine we're a writer, struggling with our latest novel. At the end of the day we realise that we've wasted our most creative hours updating and playing with our social media accounts. Can we learn from that mistake? Can we admit to ourselves that we got it wrong? We messed up and we need to get on with the important stuff? Or will we just blame writer's block or some other fictional excuse? Can we find, or do we already have, from our analysis above, something that can help us refocus our energies, to stop us from procrastinating and actually do the work? In my specific case this is the Desiderata (see below). Will we stumble around and blame the muse or actually sit down and work?

The Desiderata by Max Ehrmann is one of the things that keep me motivated each day. I've got a copy pinned above my desk at work as well as a framed piece of calligraphy on my lounge wall at home. I read it first thing in the morning and as many times as I need to keep my day on a positive footing. I guess it's a form of meditation for me. Earlier on I mentioned core values; my own core values are motivated by this poem, and it continues to motivate me daily. Find your own motivation even if it's as simple as a list of your values, or you can share mine, I'm open to that!

The Desiderata.

'Go placidly amid the noise and haste, and remember what peace
    there may be in silence.
As far as possible, without surrender, be on good terms with all persons.
Speak your truth quietly and clearly; and listen to others,
even to the dull and ignorant; they too have their story.

Avoid loud and aggressive persons, they are vexations to the spirit.
If you compare yourself with others, you may become vain or bitter,
for always there will be greater and lesser persons than yourself.
Enjoy your achievements as well as your plans.

Keep interested in your own career, however humble;
it is a real possession in the changing fortunes of time.
Exercise caution in your business affairs, for the world is full of trickery.
But let this not blind you to what virtue there is;
many persons strive for high ideals,
and everywhere life is full of heroism.

Be yourself. Especially do not feign affection. Neither be cynical about love;
for in the face of all aridity and disenchantment it is as perennial as
    the grass.
Take kindly the counsel of the years, gracefully surrendering the things
    of youth.
Nurture strength of spirit to shield you in sudden misfortune.
But do not distress yourself with dark imaginings.
Many fears are born of fatigue and loneliness.

Beyond a wholesome discipline, be gentle with yourself.
You are a child of the universe no less than the trees and the stars;
you have a right to be here. And whether or not it is clear to you,
no doubt the universe is unfolding as it should.

Therefore be at peace with God, whatever you conceive Him to be.
And whatever your labours and aspirations, in the noisy confusion of life,

> *keep peace with your soul. With all its sham, drudgery and broken dreams,*
> *it is still a beautiful world. Be cheerful. Strive to be happy.'*

Max Ehrmann 1927

The journey to self-awareness is not always easy, and we will lose some of our impetus and energy along the way, probably many times. At these times, we need to have recognized what our motivation is and be able to call on it at will in order to get back on track.

Creativity

'Creativity is intelligence having fun.' —Albert Einstein

I truly believe that everyone is creative. Even if you don't think you have a creative bone in your body, you do. There are no excuses; it's part of being human. We all just use it in different ways. It's personal to us, and there's no right or wrong way and no mistakes to be made. To some, those with a logical mind, the concept of creativity can be a mystery, but it's one worth solving.

Creativity helps us to understand ourselves on the journey to being self-aware. It can also act as a motivator and stress reducer. There we go there's the circular, web like, nature of all this again.

Me? I'm an artist. I paint, draw, design or whatever takes my fancy. I also think my other hobbies are creative too, things like cooking and gardening. They're all creative in some way. It took me a long time to recognise that not all my creative work sucks and beauty truly is in the eye of the beholder (just not mine). I used to think that my alter ego, who has to work for a living, wasn't creative at all. She's all about control, plans and time management. However, I've come to realise there's creativity even in these things. The way I have to think through problems and issues and find creative solutions. The choices I make when dealing with difficult people. I can get really creative scheduling all the tasks I have to do each day. I actually colour code my diary and to-do lists and some weeks they can look quite beautiful though I'm not sure I could ever put them on display.

Creativity is all about finding new and innovative ways to do things. There are lots of benefits to being a creative soul. It gives us balance and a sense of control (again with the control I hear you gasp). It maintains integrity, resolves conflict, and clarifies thoughts and feelings. It gives us a greater sense of well-being and personal growth. It also helps build good relationships. If we're all creative in some way, then we have common ground with everyone we have relationships with. Emotions can be creative. How we use them definitely can be. Emotions are what drive our relationships if we use them creatively there are no boundaries to what we can create between ourselves and other people. Embracing creativity minimizes our frustration at failing to find a solution to a challenge and as a result increases our productivity. To be creative, we don't need to have big ideas even the small things count. Inspiration can come from anywhere, look around you. I believe wholeheartedly in 'stealing' creatively.

Do we want to boost our latent creativity? Then we can tap into our inner child (I'm good at the whole acting like a child for the sake of being creative). Be more playful, think splatter painting with a straw and a toothbrush. Do we remember doing that as a kid? What's stopping us doing it now? Have a little fun on the way to self-awareness. My personal favorite, in the playful category, is winding people up for fun. I have to be careful not to take it too far and keep it firmly in the fun zone, and then it works for me. There are a lot of my friends out there who will attest to this, and my family certainly would.

Other ways to boost our creativity are to break habitual patterns; there's nothing worse for creativity than habit. If we're not habitual then, by default, we have to be creative. Renew an old hobby or start a new one. What made us feel good when we were kids? Why aren't we doing that now? What's stopping us from doing it again? Go on take a leap. We should expose ourselves to the arts. The term 'The Arts' describes any outlet for expression of creativity and emotion. It encompasses, but is not limited to, visual arts, performing arts, literary arts and any combination of creative outlets you care to let yourself imagine. The more we embrace any of 'the Arts' the more it rubs off on us and our creativity emerges.

We should nurture the results of our creativity, whatever they turn out to be and remember there's no right or wrong here! Just be creative.

Spirituality

'A human being is part of a whole, called by us the 'universe,' a part limited in time and space. He experiences himself, his thought and feelings, as something separate from the rest – a kind of optical delusion of his consciousness.... Our task must be to free ourselves from this prison by widening our circle of compassion to embrace all living creatures and the whole of nature in its beauty.' —Albert Einstein

I believe that spirituality is a natural human condition. I'm not talking about religion, but if that's your way of embracing your spiritual self, that's OK with me. Personally, I don't link the two, but I can take a leap and link spirituality with faith. I'm talking about the human spirit or soul as opposed to our bodies. It's self-awareness that allows us to grow our spirituality, awareness of our emotions, and physical and spiritual needs. Often the two are talked about hand in hand, and it's hard to separate them. That's OK.

From an early age we're told what to believe and follow, by parents, teachers, and even television and other media, and we do so blindly. Once the concept of self-awareness hits us, we start to question these beliefs and find our own truth, based on our understanding of ourselves, and that's exactly as it should be. All of us, who start this journey of self-awareness, have cause to question the beliefs that were instilled in us as a child. This can be the hardest part of the journey. These beliefs are deep-seated and entrenched into the very essence of us. We have grown up believing them to be the truth. The people around us believe them and therein lies the problem. We're afraid of losing the connections with other people because suddenly we no longer believe in the same things. This can be a big stumbling block.

My only advice is to look deep within ourselves. Ask the hard questions, and be brutally honest about the answers. Sometimes we have to lose connections and relationships in order to be true to ourselves and find better more rewarding ones.

Spirituality and Identifying Core Beliefs

Why is identifying core beliefs important to our spiritual lives? They are important because they lie at the centre of our soul, supporting our values and influencing our emotions.

We might decide that some of these suggestions below aren't that significant. And we would be right, to a degree. Without training our mind to see the significance of certain beliefs, they will seem unimportant. These techniques become much more powerful when coupled with awareness.

- **Listen to our 'self-talk.'** Self-talk is that constant conversation in our minds that we have with ourselves, it's the running commentary of us and our lives. Writing down the thoughts that come to our minds is a common place to start. Going back a couple of days later and reading what we wrote down is an even more effective process. The delay provides a shift in perspective that allows us to see our thoughts from a different point of view. It's this shift in point of view that's critical to seeing a belief we hold in our mind. The beliefs appear to us to be true because we've never questioned them. If we change our perspective we can see more clearly whether they're true or not and reject those that aren't. Everything appears clearer when we look back at it, and that can turn the belief into a lie. By going back and reading our thoughts, we have a better chance of finding these misrepresentations in our belief system. The thought may appear true, but behind the story is a false belief that is causing the reaction. By looking at things from a different point of view, illusions created by our minds are revealed. Discrimination is a good example of this. Discrimination often exists because that's the way we're brought up, we've lived with it through our formative years and we believe it to be the truth. Some of us recognise the lie as we mature, realising that what we always believed to be right is in fact totally wrong and we change our beliefs as a result.

- **Look at the words that we speak.** This one might sound silly because we already "know" what we say. How can we 'see' words? But we might be surprised to see the untruths and lies in those words. Many of the words we speak come out as an automatic reaction of our belief system. Being aware of our words can reveal a great deal if we know what to look for.

How many times have we said, "He/she makes me angry?" We don't control other people's emotions, so it's unlikely that others are the only factor determining what we feel inside. When we use phrases like "He/she makes me feel," we expose lies in our belief system. It's often hard to see these beliefs as lies because they appear to be true in the heat of emotion. We wrongly attribute the cause of emotion and leave it at that without paying attention to the words that come out of our mouth or the assumptions behind them. In the example 'He makes me angry' there are several questions to raise. It's a very broad statement that implies he makes us angry all the time. Is it all the time? Or is it just this one time? Are we really angry? Was this just a heat of the moment comment? Could it be that we're actually frustrated with ourselves because we don't understand where the other person is coming from? See what I mean? The comment 'He makes me angry' when looked at closely may turn out to be untrue. Once we've said it we often assume it to be true and these types of misunderstanding can taint relationships. If we 'observe' the words, we are saying we can find clues to help us identify beliefs. Seeing our thoughts and words as being false is a critical step if we're going to make any progress. There might be some resistance to this approach because our ego resists catching ourselves in a lie. Our ego insists we are always right. Let go of the ego, and we'll see we can be monumentally wrong. However, having the self-awareness to catch our mind in a lie, helps a great deal in becoming more genuine in our emotions. If that doesn't sound like much, think how it will improve all our relationships. We'll be happier, and we can then see the big benefits.

- **Finding emotions.** Being aware of our emotions is an important part of solving the puzzle of what we believe. By identifying the emotion, it's easier to see the actual belief behind it. In the above example the emotion is anger, or is it? It could be frustration with ourselves. The belief behind each is different and our reactions to it will be different. We need to understand the emotion in order to change the negative belief. Our minds work very fast, and they automatically try to lead us away from bad emotions. Trying to please others and making them feel okay doesn't stop us from feeling bad. It usually just makes us stressed. This also blinds us, so we're unaware of the beliefs and assumptions we have.

By identifying and changing the core beliefs in our mind so many of our bad emotions and behaviours go away. The first and most critical step in this process is to be aware. Taking note of what we say to ourselves, reading what we wrote, and observing the words we speak are just the beginning of the process of building self-awareness.

As we practice self-awareness, we heighten our awareness to thoughts, emotions, and core beliefs. By doing so, we see them from a different viewpoint. Then we can change them naturally. In this way, it's easy to change our beliefs. With awareness, it simply becomes common sense. If we know a belief to be a lie, then we no longer believe it. The effort involved in the process is to maintain our awareness. Once we're able to raise our awareness of the world of emotions and beliefs, we'll reap the benefits of these skills for the rest of our life and gain the motivation to keep going.

Self-awareness is gained through trial and error in focusing on the details of our personality and behaviour. As I've said before, it isn't learned from reading a book. When we read a book, we're concentrating on the ideas only. We can only gain an understanding of the ideas of self-awareness from a book. This is not the same as developing them. With our attention focused on reading, we're not paying attention to our own behaviour, emotions, and personality, so we set ourselves up to fail.

I mentioned earlier on, in ego and stress management, that meditation really helps. Anyone can meditate just don't expect to be as good as a Buddhist monk from day one. The basic technique below should be enough to see you through most of what life will throw at you.

Basic Meditation

Meditation is simple to learn but harder to perfect. Luckily a lot of the benefit comes from basic meditation. Meditation is all about closing our minds to all the 'clutter' and 'chatter' that is our normal mental world, our 'self-talk.' There should be no past or future just the here and now. It allows us to learn to focus and also relax.

If you're new to this, often the best way to start is to have one specific focus while you meditate. This can be a sound such as waves breaking, birds chirping, or a piece of music. There are plenty of ideas out there. I know this sounds clichéd, but it could be a touch. Join the tips of your middle fingers and thumbs together and concentrate on the feeling of touch between them. As you get used to concentrating on this one thing, try and concentrate on just your breathing. Notice the rhythm and the timing as you inhale and exhale, count in and out if you need to.

While you're focused, relax and ignore everything except your focal point. Do this for just five minutes a day to start and then build up to longer. See it's easy.

I meditate using these basic techniques of touch and breathing as many times a day as I feel I need to, just for five minutes at a time. It helps to refocus me back to where I should be and concentrates my time and effort.

Integrity, honesty, and personal responsibility

'Anyone who doesn't take truth seriously in small matters cannot be trusted in large ones either.' —Albert Einstein
'Waste no more time arguing about what a good man should be. Be one.' —Marcus Aurelius
'Being honest may not get you a lot of friends but it'll always get you the right ones.' —John Lennon

The message here is clear. The buck stops with us. Do not pass it on. Don't blame anyone or anything else or look for excuses. We need to make every decision with care and prove ourselves trustworthy to all those we interact with. This applies equally at work or in our personal interactions and relationships. This goes hand in hand with letting go of ego. There can't be any ego in integrity, honesty or personal responsibility.

I've said it's important to be open and honest many times already and I'll probably do so again. Honesty and therefore integrity underpin self-awareness. There is no self-awareness without them. The first person we have to be honest with is ourselves. Right at the start of this journey. Looking at our values, relationships, and beliefs. If we're not honest about the building blocks of self-awareness, then the whole concept will crumble as we try to build on it later.

As a result of our integrity, we'll attract other people with the same values as ourselves who will seek to learn from us. The more we practice it, the better we become.

If, when we're being brutally honest, we don't like ourselves we can change, one thing at a time, to do the right thing for the right reasons. Doing the right thing brings us peace and a quiet mind. To know that everything we do and say is underpinned by honesty means we never really have to think about the answers to peoples questions. The answer is always the truth which, of course, we already know by heart. So honesty protects us and gives us confidence. It helps us make better decisions and sets us apart. It creates trust and extends our influence. Once people recognise honesty and integrity in us, they will spread the word, and their respect for us will grow. This is really important if we want to succeed.

I don't think any of us deliberately set out to be dishonest most of the time. We try and be as honest as we can be given our level of self-awareness. If we don't know who we are or who we want to be then we're not being honest with ourselves, so how can we hope to be truly honest with others. Have you ever been asked by someone 'How are you?' and replied 'I'm fine,' have you been asked 'what's wrong?' and replied 'nothing.' These are knee-jerk answers, and often they are not truly honest, but we respond in that way for reasons we can't articulate. These are answers that shut down the conversation; we're saying we don't want to have that conversation on that subject. If, however, we were being truly honest then these are the conversations we should be having. Something is clearly not right or is troubling us, and we should get it out of our system by having the conversation, letting it go, and moving on.

Taking personal responsibility as part of becoming self-aware can be a painful experience for us. Quite often we discover we're not who we thought we were and not who we want to be. We have to be unconditionally honest with ourselves about this, and we have to remove self-doubt. The starting point is to take personal responsibility for our past, anything we feel guilt or shame about, act to put it right, apologise if necessary and let it go. Then we can explore how we cope with our feelings about it and learn to be grateful for the peace that comes with that.

Integrity, honesty and taking personal responsibility are the building blocks of true success. It's possible to be successful without them, but that success is hollow, has no foundation and is, therefore, shaky at best.

Giving back

'To know even one life has breathed easier because you have lived. This is to have succeeded.' —*Ralph Waldo Emerson*

This means a lot to me, I've had a lot of help in my life, particularly in my career, from people I've worked with and from total strangers, all willing to pass on their wisdom for my benefit. I've also benefitted from the little day to day kindnesses of people. I'm lucky to have friends who support me in my endeavors. There are two particular friends, who I've never actually met. We connected thanks to social media. They have supported me 100 per cent while I'm writing this book and the book is dedicated to them. Without them, this would not be happening. They both have skills and knowledge I need and cherish and are more than willing to teach me. We've probably all been on the receiving end of advice or knowledge from friends and colleagues, and we have probably benefitted from it as well. It's only right that we share our own knowledge, expertise, and skills with others who come after us. This helps them, as well as balancing our life; it's karma.

Sharing and giving back increases our happiness and health, it makes us feel good about ourselves. Sharing promotes cooperation and social connection, and it evokes gratitude. Last but not least it's contagious. If we share for the benefit of others, then those we share with will be more likely to share and pass those benefits on. Think what we could achieve if we could get a few snowballs going.

There are lots of ways to give back and even the little things count. One of my values is to do a good deed every day. When we're waiting in line at the coffee shop, pay for the coffee of the person behind us. When we're planting spring bulbs in our gardens save some, and go and plant them along the roadsides (where we're allowed to!) so others can benefit from them. On a larger scale, if you have experience and knowledge that others would benefit from, pass it on, and mentor the next generation. We all have something to give back.

There are countless volunteer organisations out there who are crying out for people to help and support them. Some enlightened businesses allow their staff a few days a year, paid, to volunteer at local charities. I'm lucky enough to work for one such organisation.

I'm grateful that I'm able to give back in some small way. It feels like closing the circle of life and making things complete. It feels good even without the help of my dreaded ego.

Summary of self-awareness

Self-awareness is not about reading a book or attending a course. Self-awareness is a journey, and it takes practice. It's like a muscle that becomes more effective with time and effort. It gives us mental strength as opposed to physical strength. We are constantly changing and adapting to the multiple external forces around us and to our individual experiences. The more we learn to be aware of, and understand, our reactions, thoughts, and emotions, while also keeping in mind our values, the more we can become the best we can be and the more successful we can become.

Finally, I've included below twelve things we can do that can help us on the journey towards greater self-awareness. These things help reinforce this message. We don't have to do any of them, but they can help us if we do.

- **Ask ourselves why three times.** Before we make any important decisions ask why? Then ask why again and then again. If, after asking why three times, we've come up with three good reasons to make the decision then we should go for it. This reasoning process and subsequent answers give us clarity as to whether the decision is the right one or not and therefore gives us confidence we're doing the right thing. It's like listening to a child asking 'why' so many times and on this journey it often feels as though we're children embarking on something new and exciting and yet unknown.
- **Talk about our emotions.** Emotions cause powerful physical and behavioral reactions, and are more complex than just "happy" or "angry." Putting our feelings into words is good for us. If we're unable to understand and explain how we feel, that can cause us stress. We need to be able to talk about our emotions.
- **Learn to say no to ourselves.** The ability to say no to ourselves is an important skill. Again, like a muscle, it's strengthened with exercise. The more we practice saying no to the small things, the better we can withstand big temptations. Think about the temptations that are put in front of us every day, social media, junk food, and gossiping to name but three. Try to say no to as many a day as possible. This is so hard for me that I end up with precious few no's but I'm persistent. I keep trying.

- **Stop knee-jerk reactions.** A person without self-awareness reacts according to habit and responds with knee-jerk reactions. Self-awareness allows us to assess the situation objectively and rationally, without acting out of habit and learned responses. To do this, we need to take a deep breath before we do anything, especially when a situation evokes a negative emotion such as anger or frustration. This gives us time to re-assess whether our response is the best one and then make the right choice. I'm going to have to hold my hands up here and admit that I'm not as good at this as I would like to be.

- **Be aware of our weaknesses.** We're not perfect. Being aware of our weaknesses, but failing to accept the responsibility, is not the way forward. We often criticise others, while being closed off to our own shortcomings. Self-awareness helps shine a light on ourselves and prevents us being hypocrites. Self-awareness only happens when we acknowledge our weaknesses. We must acknowledge our shortcomings rather than excuse our reactions to them. As I said above one of my failings is a tendency to react too fast to strong emotions such as anger. I acknowledge this but that doesn't excuse it, it's wrong. I need to work through alternative responses and try not to let this define me. It's a recognized weakness.

- **Manage the noise in our heads.** The noise in our heads is not always helpful. At best it can be distracting, but at worst a little bit of negativity can soon get out of control and turn into stress. For this reason, we need to pay attention to the way we respond to our successes and failures. We shouldn't assume our successes are due to luck; they're due to our hard work. We should never beat ourselves up over our failures. Good and bad feelings take shape in our minds based on how we react to success and failure. Being tough on ourselves needs to be balanced with self-compassion. We should celebrate our wins and forgive our losses. If we can do this, we'll be much happier.

- **Improve our non-verbal communication awareness.** Perhaps the best way to learn about body language is to video ourselves. Sorry, but in the interest of honesty and personal integrity, no I'm not doing that. Awareness of our body language and posture improves our confidence. Bad body language causes negativity, standing up straight improves our outlook on everything. Using hand gestures helps articulate our thoughts and affects how people respond to us. If we record ourselves and assess our posture and hand gestures we can learn a lot about ourselves. If we then watch videos of skilled speakers and adopt their mannerisms to improve our own, we can learn even more

- **Play devil's advocate.** Taking an opposing view, with our own thoughts, forces us to question our assumptions about ourselves. Our first thoughts and views are not always the best or the most accurate. It's good to argue with ourselves and see how our views hold up. We can learn a lot about ourselves this way.

- **Knowing our personality type.** I covered the various personality types earlier and knowing our personality type allows us to play to our strengths and manage our weaknesses. Understanding our strengths and talents can make the difference between a good choice, and a great choice. Strengths are skills and knowledge that can be acquired, while talents are innate so be aware of the difference.

- **Getting regular feedback.** It's hard for us to understand all of our thinking patterns and behavior. Getting regular feedback improves our awareness, but we should only ask those people who understand us and whom we respect. Make sure they're the type of person who will tell us what we need to hear, not what we want to hear. We can learn some tough lessons here, but if we're aware, then we can understand that we need to do this to improve.

- **Regular self-evaluation and reflection.** It's a good idea to keep a diary to track our progress. We need to know our current level of self-awareness. We can also track how often we stray from the path and do things we regret or make knee-jerk decisions. If we set regular small goals, we can check how well we're doing on a daily basis. Then we can set goals to improve day by day.

- **Practice Meditation.** As I said in a previous section meditation is an important practice for improving self-awareness. To focus solely on our breathing is to focus on an important body process. We'll become aware of how our mind wanders, and get better at ignoring distractions. I've included the basics of meditation earlier on in this book.

Why should we develop self-awareness?

Some people think the idea of changing our emotional reactions, the way we behave, or our belief is tough to do. Trying to change our beliefs, particularly those that were enforced on us years ago, can be challenging. We need to take action that may feel uncomfortable and spend time practicing. What is hard is to spend the rest of our lives limited by fear and emotional reactions that have accumulated since childhood. That's not the way I want to live.

When we start to think about self-awareness, commonly the first question we ask is "What's wrong with me?" The truth is 'nothing,' we're fine. There really is nothing wrong with us. The next question is: "I don't feel fine. Why do I feel so unhappy, angry, sad, etc.?" This is because the emotions we feel are created as reactions to beliefs we have and our beliefs may be negative therefore our emotions react accordingly. Our emotions are responding to what is going on in our mind. The problem is that we have negative thoughts in our mind and we believe them. How we feel emotionally is just a response to those beliefs. The important thing to understand is that we're not the issue. There's nothing wrong with us; it's what's going on in our mind that's the issue. Once we buy into that, it becomes really easy.

As we become more comfortable with self-awareness, we start to make changes in our thoughts and our interpretation of those thoughts. Changing the way we interpret our thoughts allows us to change our emotional reactions. Self-awareness is one of the key areas of emotional intelligence and an important factor in achieving success. We do want to be successful, Right?

We all want to get a grip on our lives and understand exactly what it is we want. Self-awareness is the first step in doing this. Where we apply our focus, emotions, reactions, personality, and behaviour determines our direction in life. If we're self-aware, we can see where our thoughts and emotions are taking us and apply some control allowing us to change them as we go. Until we're self-aware, we'll struggle to make positive changes in the direction of our life. When we become self-aware, we understand all the judgments, opinions, thoughts, and beliefs that our mind deals with. We can then see how much this influences our emotions, though not always in a positive way. These emotional reactions are the things we can most easily change. Once we take fear out of the equation, and hence a lot of negative emotional baggage it becomes easier.

Developing our sense of self-awareness is a way to bring happiness into our lives. One key message here is *we* don't have to change, we are not the problem. It's our mind and all the negative thoughts and emotions and our interpretation of these that's the issue.

Even the question, *"What is wrong with me?"* is built on the assumptions that:

- There is something wrong with us in the first place
- We don't know what's wrong with us
- We should know what's wrong with us, but we don't

All of these assumptions make us worry that there's something wrong with us. Yes, we feel bad, but that's because we're caught up in these assumed beliefs that there's something wrong. It's a stupid question, and we shouldn't be wasting our time trying to answer it.

The intention here is to get rid of the fear and limiting beliefs that create unhappiness in us and our relationships. As a result this can help us stop our emotional reactions and control the thoughts in our mind. Also it helps us identify and change the beliefs behind our thoughts and emotions and shifts our point of view to see our self and others differently. We can then begin to ignore the voice in our head, the 'self-talk,' that is critical of us and others and ultimately develop respect for our self and other people. We also gain control over our thoughts so we can focus on creating love and happiness in our life, and in our relationships.

Is this too much to reach for? Not if we understand that most of our negative thoughts, attitude, emotions, and behaviour arise from our beliefs. Whether our specific issue is insecurity, fear of public speaking, jealousy, anger, controlling behaviour, or something else, it is founded on our beliefs. Once we develop our awareness and the skills to change our beliefs, then changing our thoughts, emotional reaction, and behavior becomes easier.

Summary of actions from this section:

- Remove our ego.
- Focus on our relationships and building empathy.
- Manage our stress.
- Recognise our motivation.
- Be creative.
- Identify and understand our beliefs.
- Learn to meditate.
- Build our integrity.
- Give back where we can.
- Continue the journey to self-awareness.

Chapter 2

EMOTIONAL AWARENESS

'I don't want to be at the mercy of my emotions. I want to use them, to enjoy them, and to dominate them.' —*Oscar Wilde*
'People will forget what you do, people will forget what you say, but people will never forget how you made them feel.' —*Maya Angelou*

Introduction to emotion

We're now all self-aware. Right? We've gone through all the actions in the previous section, and we're now in a position to look at emotional awareness. I've written about emotions a lot in the previous section as they form part of self-awareness so now is the time to look more closely at them and to understand them a bit better. The title of this section is very presumptuous as if I need to introduce any of you to emotion. Or do I?

Emotional awareness means being able to recognise emotions that we experience, understand the feelings associated with those emotions, and understand what we think and do as a result, in other words how we react.

Emotion is an important player in our ability to think positively, after all, it's what drives us as human beings. I don't intend to cover the whole range of possible emotions here, no one would ever be able to finish the book, but I'll pick a few that mean something to me. Emotion is not something we can switch on and off. It's not something we can force ourselves to embrace. It simply is. In any given situation we either feel it, or we don't. However, there are things we can do to put ourselves in the path of certain emotions and also to manage how we react to them. We

54

have to understand our emotions and those of others and not only how, but why, we react to them the way we do. Then, and only then, can we regulate and control those reactions.

Go back to self-awareness for a minute. If we know, understand, and recognise our triggers then we know what triggers our emotions. If we make sure we're subjected to those triggers we can feel those emotions, simple, right? If I'm sad, for whatever reason, then going on the internet and looking up silly cat videos always makes me happy. Not all the emotions are that easy to change, but the principle still works. If I'm feeling any kind of negative emotion I go and read The Desiderata and I feel instantly uplifted and at peace with the world. That's what I mean by putting ourselves in the path of certain emotions.

Emotional awareness (as opposed to self-awareness)

Emotional awareness is a big part of self-awareness. We can't have one without the other. It's all about our ability to recognise our own emotions and their effects on us. If we have the ability to be emotionally aware we know what emotions we're feeling at all times, and why. We also understand the links between our emotions and our thoughts and actions. This includes what we say and do, and means we also understand how our feelings will affect those actions.

It's very important to our own well-being and happiness to be aware of our emotions and how they affect us. It's crucial to enable us to have good relationships with others. We sometimes hide our emotions rather than expressing them, and this leads us to develop ways to distract ourselves, so that we don't have to cope with those emotions. Self-analysis of emotions can be a challenge particularly if those emotions have been repressed or hidden for some time. We may not be able to immediately recognise those emotions for what they are let alone stand a chance of understanding them and why they make us feel the way they do. However, self-analysis is a vital skill to develop in order to have good emotional awareness.

To start, as with self-awareness, we need to be aware of our personal values because they also have emotional value to us. Our emotional reactions are as a result of any impacts to our personal values, which, if you remember, we defined at the start of self-awareness. If we're aware of our values, then we can understand our emotional reaction to them and therefore be emotionally aware.

Understanding our own emotions, and those of others requires an understanding of our strengths, weaknesses, and, perhaps most importantly, our limits. As I've said before it can be particularly hard to admit to weaknesses and therefore our limits, especially if we're in an environment where it's frowned upon, but it's important for emotional awareness and our own well-being. We need to be aware that there can be areas which we cannot see, (remember our unknown self?) such as goals that are unrealistic, needing to be always right and lack of work life balance. These hidden areas can make us resistant to hearing the truth about ourselves. It's therefore even more important to get regular feedback from people we trust to be honest with us so that we can acknowledge this and act on it. People who are good at self-assessment generally have a good understanding of their strengths and weaknesses, a good sense of humour about themselves, and their limitations. This really helps. If we start to feel negative emotions at this stage it's going to be even tougher to become emotionally aware so we can learn to like what we see and if we don't then we can learn to change it.

Applying reason to emotion

As I've said, we can't change how we feel we can only change how we respond. The important thing to remember is to be aware of our emotional reactions, and also be able to understand what triggers them. That way, we can apply some reason and logic to the situation. For example, we might ask ourselves some questions about courses of action we can take. How do we feel about a situation and what do we think we should do about it? What effect would that action have on us and other people? Does that action fit with our values and if not, what else could we do that might fit better? Is there anyone else that we could ask about this who might help us?

I'll use an example to illustrate this. Imagine a friend has accused me, unjustly, of something. I'm feeling angry and hurt, and my instinct is to hit back and argue. I realise I must stop, breathe and think about it. Acting that way would almost certainly ruin our relationship and end up hurting both of us even more. That reaction also doesn't fit with my personal values. Instead, I look at what happened and what was said to see if I misunderstood or misinterpreted it and to assess whether I overreacted. I'll talk it through hypothetically with another friend to check my assumptions. As a result, I decide to explain to the friend that accused me that what he did hurt me and that I don't understand why but that if he feels that way about it I'll accept his feelings and try to understand. I'll ask that we let it go and move on.

This can help us apply reason to an emotional reaction before we actually react.

When we make decisions, we can draw on reason and emotion, or a mixture of the two. Emotional decisions can be seen as being made in the 'heat of the moment,' but emotions play a large part in almost all of our decisions. It's also important to understand that decisions are not made solely on the basis of reason. The best decisions are made using both logic and emotion. If we only use one or the other, our decisions will not be balanced, or not support our emotional needs. Instead, we need to combine our emotional reaction with more logical thought. We can do this by stopping before we decide, to give ourselves a chance to think about our reactions. Thinking about how we will feel as a result of an action, thinking about what might happen as a result of our actions, and how our decision might affect others. We could ask ourselves whether we would be happy with the impacts. We could also consider our values and whether the decision fits with them.

Now that we're aware of the key concepts in understanding our emotions and emotional awareness, we can take a closer look at some of the most powerful emotions that drive our lives.

Love

'When we feel love and kindness toward others, it not only makes others feel loved and cared for, but it helps us also to develop inner happiness and peace.' —Dalai Lama XIV

This has to be included as number one in this section; I am, and always will be, in love with love. Love is fulfilling, exciting, and good for us. It leads to sharing of other emotions and life experiences. The dictionary definition doesn't do it justice 'warm liking or affection for a person' boring words for something so passionate and all consuming. I couldn't function without the love of my family and friends or without being able to love the other passions in my life, my cats, art and good books.

Love (not just sex although that works too) releases Oxytocin into our systems 'the cuddle chemical' which reduces pain and increases energy and alertness. What better reason do we need? We learn to love from building relationships with others, and that enriches our lives. In return, we gain increased emotional health. It helps us practice generosity, forgiveness, patience, and acceptance. When we have love in our lives, we are far more open to all the other positive emotions as well. Wow, all those positive emotions just from love! We really need love in our lives.

Love makes the world go round, doesn't it? Wars are fought in its name and murders committed because of it. Hang on; those are very negative actions for such a positive emotion. On the other hand families and friends bond in the name of it. People do the most amazing things when they are 'in love.' It makes us smile and laugh and enjoy life and isn't that what it's all about? OK, I'm looking at it through rose coloured glasses, I recognise that love is not always reciprocated and when it's not it can be hell, I know, I've been there, along with a good many of you as well I imagine. But when love is two-way, life is good. When we're in love and are loved back, do we need a book to help us? No, we don't, it comes naturally, and that's my point, love really can help us all to think more positively. I'm lucky to have really good friends that I love and that I know love me in return. I also have a loving family that I would do anything for. Why? Because I love them, of course, and that love is unconditional.

The benefits of love don't have to come just from the love between people. Think outside the simple dictionary definition. I love art; it gives me pleasure to look at it, to try and understand the thought behind it, it makes me think, which increases my focus and energy levels. I love creating art both for my own pleasure and the enjoyment of others. I love my cats; they give me immeasurable pleasure, and they make me laugh which again makes me feel good. I love reading and enjoying the fruits of someone else's creativity.

Everyone would love to know the secret to finding love, but it can't be found it has to be experienced and realised within ourselves. Before we can love another person we have to love ourselves. How can we understand the ways in which this incredible emotion affects how we feel about someone else. That's very easy to say, but actually, if we look with self-awareness at ourselves, it's not so easy to do. Self-awareness can help us learn to love ourselves. It helps us change into a person we value and want to be, and once that happens it's easy to love ourselves.

Our spirit, or soul, is filled with all the intuition and wisdom born from emotions such as love. It's what tells us when we are making bad decisions, and it learns from emotion. The other side of this is our ego, which I spoke of earlier, which learns from our experiences in life. If we can balance the two or squash our ego enough, then we open ourselves up to the emotional side such as compassion, gratitude, forgiveness and, yes, love, even love for ourselves.

Love is a noun, but it's also a verb. If we show and express love to the next generation, they will grow up with a natural ability to show love themselves. Children are emotionally expressive; they don't care what other people think. As we grow up, it's far more difficult to be genuine about who we are and how we feel, particularly for those coming to terms with whom they are and how they fit into a society with rigid belief systems. For those that don't fit in often the only way forward is to live on the edge of society not showing their true selves, which is so sad. This can be particularly true when the cause of the isolation is sexual orientation, where the edges of society become the 'closet.' As adults looking into self-awareness, we can try to get back some of our childish ability to show our genuine feelings, including love. Maintaining a positive outlook helps on our path to true love. I'm not saying it's easy when sharing our real feelings leads to potential societal abuse.

Self-awareness tells us to concentrate on the positives in our values and beliefs so one of our positives may be 'I am ready and open to fall in love with the right person.' We should always focus on what we want and then plan to act on it. If we want to fall in love and we plan for doing it then when the right person crosses our path we're ready. If we don't acknowledge that we're ready then love might just pass us by without us even noticing it.

Earlier I spoke about 'self-talk' and listening to ourselves and maybe even writing down what we're telling ourselves. This is the time to ensure that those conversations with ourselves are positive and not negative. How can we expect to attract the love of our lives with negative thoughts rumbling around inside our heads? We can challenge those negative thoughts and replace them with positive ones in order to be ready to embrace that love when it arrives. One of the important messages about positive thoughts is to forgive past loves. Let go of any bitterness or regret and move on. If we can't move on from the past, then we can't embrace the love here in the present or in the future. We need to be sending out the right messages. Remember I said earlier to live in the present? This is our chance to put that into practice. If we're positive in our values and the way we live we'll attract positive people. We could be missing out on 'the one' simply by being too negative. Being positive means, we'll be remembered positively. We can all choose to be that way using what we've learned about self-awareness. Beware, though, if you're not being genuine about this, your body language may just give you away. Other people will pick up on the mismatch between what you say and what your body is saying.

Let's take a minute to recap on some of the messages from self-awareness to ensure we understand how we can change and become positive in order to embrace love. If we're self-aware, we manage our negative emotions and particularly our reactions to them. We help others starting with family and friends and then strangers. We make sure our values and goals stand up to scrutiny and don't contradict each other. Above all we remember all the benefits of self-awareness.

If we follow the path of self-awareness and practice it, then there's absolutely no reason we can't love ourselves and as a result find the love that we are looking for in our lives. If we want love, we should first learn to give love.

Never underestimate the power of this emotion to change the way we perceive things and to change our lives for the better. Go and put yourself in the path of love at every opportunity.

Passion

'My mission in life is not merely to survive, but to thrive;
and to do so with some passion, some compassion, some
humour, and some style.' —Maya Angelou

Maybe I should have lumped this in with love, but I didn't, and deliberately so. I wanted to keep it separate because passion can be felt without love. Love can be passive and gentle, but passion is strong and fierce. When we feel passion, in its positive sense, it brings energy and creates change. It ignites others with its contagious nature and drives vision. It's an unstoppable force of nature, and we *must* go with the flow and see where it leads us.

It's a sad fact that as children we're far more passionate about things than we are when we grow up. As we become adults, we lose the natural passion we had as children. Sometimes it's actually 'beaten' out of us by people telling us we can't do or achieve what we want to. Sometimes it's just a slow recognition of our responsibilities as a grown up that causes passion to just slip away. If we think about what still excites or excited us when we were younger then maybe we can get some passion back into our lives. It's got to be worth a try.

Passion is not just felt for the people in our lives although we should all experience that side of it at least once. Passion can be felt for objects, situations, ideas, the list is endless, and therefore the passion is potentially endless too. What a fantastic thought! Think of the passion felt by people who are part of national or international movements for change or that exhibited by environmental activists. To be a world-class athlete takes passion as well as commitment. Scholars have a passion for their chosen subjects and move the world forward for the better. Artists, working in all types of media, have a passion for their creations and also the passion to share them with us. Thank you to them all for doing just that.

I feel passionate about our world, the earth we live on. I studied Geography at university, which perhaps gives me a bit more insight than some. Even without that extra knowledge we can feel the passion for this beautiful planet. It's not about what we know but about what we feel! Feelings don't need facts to have a positive influence on us. We don't need to understand the different biological mechanisms at work in a tropical rainforest in order to be able to see it as a wonderful thing of beauty. We don't need to understand the climatic conditions required to create a rainbow in order to stand and stare at the colours with awe.

We should never let the passion in our lives wane. I was guilty of this once upon a time and life became just shades of gray and not the fifty kinds either. I was lucky enough to have, and be able to connect with, beautiful friends who dragged me back up and literally put the passion back into my life (no not like that!) they showed me how to enjoy living again for which I will be eternally grateful. They know who they are!

As with love, thinking positively can help us to discover passion. If we live life with passion and enjoy everything, then we live life with purpose. Then we're more likely to achieve success. The sorry truth though is that most of us don't live this way all the time. We don't always enjoy life. Part of the reason for this is, not really knowing what we want out of life. This is where self-awareness helps us to define what we want and how we can get it. It helps us to ignore all the preconceived ideas and beliefs about why we can't do it. Throwing away all the negative thoughts and embracing our lives with renewed passion. Of course, we have to really want it and believe that we can do it, reaffirming it with positive thinking. As we do this, we naturally start to believe in ourselves, and the path to getting what we want becomes easier. We just need to do it with passion.

Optimism and hope

'I am an optimist. It does not seem too much use being anything else.' —*Winston Churchill*

Being optimistic means we expect the best possible outcome from any situation. Both optimism and pessimism are concerned with our view of the future but are coloured by our experiences of the past. There is virtue everywhere we look and in everything we see. Sometimes we have to look hard, and it may be deeply hidden away, but I promise you it's there. Optimists (and I include myself here) are glass half full people, and we believe negative situations are short term. Yes, I get down like anyone else but I time box it and let it go, and before long I'm back up on top of it again. Hope gives us a reason for living; it's positive anticipation of the future.

I'll give you a personal example. I hope a couple of friends will be able to come over to Britain from America to visit me in the future. I'm optimistic they'll make it and thinking about it makes me feel fantastic. They've never been here before, and I'm already planning everywhere I want to take them and all the sights I think they'll want to see. I'm positively looking forward to a future event. Nothing has been booked, and they haven't said they're definitely coming but my life feels better just because of hope, and I feel lighter as a result of my optimism. Of course, I'm also self-aware, so I recognise the possibility of any negative thoughts and emotions, such as disappointment, if my friends don't come to visit. As a result of this awareness, I can also understand my possible reactions to these negative emotions. I can be prepared with ways to avoid them or be able to time box them. I hope I don't need to.

What are the benefits of being an optimist? It reduces stress, allowing us to be better able to handle emotions. It promotes happiness and self-respect as well as integrity. It also gives a sense of fulfillment and satisfaction. In turn, this leads to increased productivity and ability to deal with failure. If we're optimistic, we believe we can turn around failure and make it into success. We work harder at everything because we believe in a positive outcome and working harder makes us more likely to succeed.

Until I saw the benefits of being an eternal optimist, I was unable to deal with failure or criticism. I'm what they call a high achiever and haven't had much exposure to either. I never had the opportunity when I was younger to grow a thick skin. As a result, my first experiences of failure laid me flat, and I can tell you I didn't like it! Needless to say, I can cope better now. I can see criticism as an opportunity to change myself for the better and I can see failure as a chance to learn valuable lessons for the future. I've learned from my failures and grown stronger and more resilient as a result.

Optimism helps give us patience. We can wait a long time if we know the result is going to be good. It makes us proactive and helps balance our life with increased peace of mind and a positive attitude. Increased motivation is a side effect of hope. We want to see a positive outcome which in turn motivates us to do whatever it takes to get it. Optimism is always constructive; optimism never destroyed anything. It increases good relationships and rubs off on those we come into contact with. It also builds resilience, self-confidence, and self-esteem as well as helping us focus. That's got to be good motivation for being an optimist.

However, there's always a 'but.' We must set realistic goals and expectations with the emphasis on realistic. If we start with unrealistic expectations, we're heading for a disaster. We should be honest with ourselves about what we can change and achieve and then we'll achieve it easily. That doesn't mean our goals can't be stretching. In fact, it's better if they are. If we can achieve our goals without really trying, there's no motivation to improve ourselves. We can learn from the past, but we must manage the present for a better future. With optimism and hope, we can do that and achieve our dreams.

It's OK to fail or make mistakes so long as we learn from it, thank goodness. Believe me, I've made some monumentally large mistakes, but I've still managed to turn things around and come out with even more optimism and hope than I had before. How? I learned from them and became aware of changes I needed to make and then I made them. I'm not saying I've never made the same mistake twice, but I'd like to think the triggers were different in each case, so I was unable to recognise them before it was too late. That's my excuse anyway.

Having waxed lyrical about the benefits of being an optimist it's very easy to slide from optimism into denial of the truth; we need to look at things with open eyes. It's good to be an optimist but not if it blinds us to the truth. This is where self-awareness comes into its own. We have to balance our optimism with a healthy dose of reality in order to maintain some balance. If we only believe in optimism without reality, then we actually miss out on a lot of opportunities to learn and grow. We can also prevent bad things from tripping us up if we recognise that they're there. If we're over-optimistic, we can also come across as overconfident and assume we don't need to change things, when in reality we do, in order to prevent bad outcomes. If we combine optimism with the honesty to clearly see what's going on around us, then we can maintain that healthy balance. If the truth is good, then we actually don't need optimism. Using optimism to focus on an illusion blinds us from seeing reality and prevents us from putting things right, learning from mistakes and moving forward. A common example of this is being in an unhappy relationship, a part of us knows that it's wrong. If we're an eternal optimist we'll be hoping that things will change and telling ourselves it's all OK when it's not. I know, I've been there. When reality finally hits us, then we're likely to be more hurt than if we'd done something about it earlier. We've probably all done something like this, but with self-awareness we can apply realism and hope never to do it again.

We're not born being optimistic or pessimistic both are acquired through experiencing life. They are intrinsically linked to self-awareness and our need to find out the truth about ourselves. The less we know about ourselves, the less confident we are. This leads us to negative thoughts because of our uncertainty. If we're not self-aware, it's easy to think the world is not treating us fairly and this can lead to anger and pessimism. Pessimism is also a de-motivator. I warned you this was all linked.

Although there's no scientific evidence to show that optimists feel less pain or get ill less, there are signs that they tend to be more emotionally well-adjusted and cope with bad circumstances better. Optimism can improve our health through the benefits of positive thinking. The fact that optimists experience less stress and are less likely to give up supports this.

Most successful people see the opportunities in every situation rather than the difficulties. So long as our optimism is not unrealistic, then it can give us the power to be confident and overcome any difficulties that arise.

If we want to become an optimist a good place to start is with the successes and failures in our lives. We need to understand how we felt and what emotions we were experiencing at the time. Once we understand that, we can think about how we can change it. What we learn this way can ensure we think positively even about our failures. We can also look at the people around us, who we know help us and teach us to grow. Look at whether they are optimists or pessimists. Just thinking positively won't make it happen but it will help us to see the opportunities given to us. Optimists and pessimists approach things differently, but optimists are more able to cope successfully with difficult events. They recover from disappointments more quickly and are generally happier with their lives. This could be because they're more likely to look for solutions to problems when faced with setbacks.

Gratitude is a trait linked to people who are optimistic, and the benefits of that can be seen later.

Optimism has been shown to protect us from depression, and recent research shows that optimism can possibly be learned through Cognitive Behavioural Therapy, or CBT. If so we can all benefit from it. Even coloured with a healthy dose of realism it pays to be an optimist in life. The benefits clearly outweigh the downsides.

Happiness

'I believe that the very purpose of life is to be happy. From the very core of our being, we desire contentment....I have found that the more we care for the happiness of others, the greater is our own sense of well-being.' —Dalai Lama XIV

Happy people are more successful, get less sick, have more friends, are more helpful, have a positive influence on others, smile more, live longer, are more proactive, productive, and creative. Gosh, that's a heady list of benefits, but I think the topic speaks for itself. We should aspire to be happy for as large a percentage of our time as we can. Is it possible to be happy all the time? Probably not, but it's fun trying.

Being an optimist, I find it hard not to be happy, but it can and does happen. I have a rolling list in my head (more about my ability to run my life with lists later) of things that make me happy, friends, memories, family, and pets. If I need a boost to my happiness, I need only to turn to this list, and it makes me happy.

I am going to call out my Somali cat, Nismo, here because since he arrived two and a half years ago there hasn't been a single day when he hasn't made us laugh in some way or another. He doesn't bring in birds or mice; he collects sticks, twigs and leaves (the latter get stuck to his coat, and he brings them indoors by default) he's a nature lover! He doesn't curl up in a neat ball like other cats; he sprawls, usually on his back with his feet in the air. The contorted positions he prefers to sleep in have had us staring hard and trying to figure out which way round various bits are. We have come to the conclusion that he's articulated in the middle, much like a truck. Can you figure out the picture?

I've got a video of Nismo as a kitten; he's in a shoe box chasing my sons' finger. He suddenly reaches up with a paw and grabs the edge of the lid of the box, pulls it down and tucks it in the bottom, effectively shutting himself in. If I ever need a laugh, I go back and play the video, and it always lifts my spirits. Nismo is a happy cat!

Once we're happy, how do we stay happy? Easy, we practice good self-awareness. We let negative things go, cherish our relationships, love our passions, manage our stress, keep ourselves motivated and healthy, embrace our creativity and grow our spirituality. Everything I've been talking about up to this point leads to happiness.

We'd all like to be happy and have a positive view of life, but we can easily be drawn into negative thoughts. We can turn this around and live focused on the good rather than the bad. We can ensure that the things we do lean towards positive emotions. We can read uplifting books, listen to music that makes us happy, and surround ourselves with happy, supportive people. I can think of five steps we can all take to lead a happier life that have a basis in self-awareness.

- **Believing that happiness is a choice.** We can start by believing that happiness is a choice. We can stop blaming forces outside of our control for the way we feel and instead choose how we want to feel. It really is up to us to take control and find the good in everything. Please note this is one of my core values.
- **Get rid of the negative 'stuff'.** We can get rid of negative 'stuff' in our lives (also a core value of mine). We can avoid negative people and things by assessing what makes us feel negative about it and then getting rid of the triggers.
- **Looking for the positives.** Having got rid of the negatives, we can actively look for the positives. We can learn to focus on the good in every situation even though sometimes we may have to look hard. Sometimes it's easy to let a negative feeling take root simply because it takes effort to change it. At the very least we can always learn from a negative experience, and that's good.
- **Regularly enforcing our optimism.** We can make sure our own optimism is regularly enforced. We can practice being in a good mood. We can be positive about who we are and what we achieve

and praise ourselves for doing well. We don't have to be positive about everything but we mustn't think about the negatives too much.

- **Sharing our happiness.** Finally, we can share our happiness with others. We can be nice to everyone we meet whether it's deserved or not. Tell people we love them or are grateful for them. We mustn't be critical although we can offer critique. We should treat people as we want to be treated.

If changing from being negative to being positive feels like a long, hard road then go back and review the benefits of being happy. We can be self-aware and believe in ourselves and tell ourselves that being happy is a choice.

Humour

'When his life was ruined, his family killed, his farm destroyed, Job knelt down on the ground and yelled up to the heavens, 'Why God? Why me?' and the thundering voice of God answered, 'There's just something about you that pisses me off.' —Stephen King

Please, please, please, we shouldn't take ourselves too seriously. I don't take myself seriously at all so maybe I've gone to the other extreme but better that than the alternative. Smile and laugh, a lot. I know it's corny, but laughter really is the best medicine, and you don't have to take my word for it, look at the number of sites on the web for jokes, funny pictures, silly articles and loads more. Oh, you have! Good, then you know what I'm talking about. I have a particularly well developed and ever so slightly warped sense of humour (OK, I can hear my friend's intake of breath there, it's very warped). I don't find things funny that other people do but I do find humour in the strangest, possibly abnormal, places. Oh, and I have a dirty mind, so innuendo works for me as does farce. I'm not justifying or excusing it; I love being that way, it makes life fun.

The benefits of humour really can't be overemphasised. It strengthens the immune system, boosts energy, lessens pain, reduces stress, relaxes our muscles, lowers blood pressure and relieves tension. Laughter makes us feel good. It also has a powerful positive effect on our bodies and our mental and spiritual health and these benefits also extend to others. That really should be enough to make us use it more often! It's a powerful tool and one that's with us all the time. We don't even have to take it out of the tool box!

Humour is powerful enough that it can change the attitudes of others. There's nothing like a well-placed joke or funny story in the middle of the driest presentation to make people sit back up in their seats and take notice. So don't do it just for yourself, make someone else laugh! Spread the happiness.

Humour and laughter can be used to reaffirm our mental health. Laughter can help us overcome challenges and put them in perspective. It gives us a more light-hearted view of events making them less threatening. It improves our mood and helps us feel better about ourselves. It can also distract us from stressful situations by forcing us to focus away from negative emotions. It also connects us with others. If someone smiles at us, it's hard not to smile back and as we all know laughter really is infectious. By laughing we not only reduce our own stress levels but those of the people around us by allowing us to forget about our problems for a while.

Humour can also open us up to a more spiritual awareness of life. By removing bad thoughts, we clear our minds and meditation becomes easier and more effective. Communication becomes easy through shared humour, and we feel closer to those people with whom we've shared a good belly laugh. We can help build new relationships and strengthen old ones by having a sense of humour and also get to know like-minded people. Humour can lower our resistance to scary challenges such as meeting new people, it can, in other words, also be used to 'break the ice.'

Humour is attractive and laughing will attract people to us. More importantly, those people will also have a sense of humour and therefore enrich our lives helping us to stay positive. It's human nature to enjoy laughing and if it has beneficial effects such as stress reduction that's even better. A good sense of humour can help us laugh at challenges and diffuse anger. Can we really stay angry at someone who makes us laugh?

Humour is one of those emotions which help us with emotional awareness by putting us in the right frame of mind to become aware of good things and ignore the bad ones. So go on, laugh.

Compassion

'Compassion... is human business, it is not luxury, it is essential for our own peace and mental stability, it is essential for human survival.' —Dali Lama XI

Whereas humour helps us on the path to self-awareness, Compassion forces us to be self-aware. Showing compassion is never a bad thing. Compassion is seeing things from another's perspective and experiencing empathy. It literally means to suffer with others. This is the opposite side of the emotional wheel to selfishness. To be truly compassionate about someone else entails a certain amount of compassion for ourselves as well so don't underestimate this emotion. We should allow ourselves to be compassionate to ourselves. It's part of being self-aware.

Compassion for others makes us happy; it actually activates pleasure centres in our brains having a positive effect on self-esteem. It can also lower our heart rate and reduce stress. It makes us attractive to others and uplifts them and us. It's highly contagious just like other positive emotions because, like love, it involves our hearts. It's also natural and human. It forces engagement with our surroundings, environment, and life in general and makes communication and relating to others easier. Societies which are more compassionate tend to be happier and live longer.

Compassion encompasses acts of kindness, care and support and a whole raft of other actions and thoughts. It can be as small as a smile or as large as trekking halfway around the world to help people less fortunate than ourselves. It can only be authentic; we can't fake it easily. It focuses us beyond ego and into our own self-awareness.

Compassion is often linked with empathy or sympathy, but the latter two are only related to feelings whereas compassion encompasses action to help. It is this need to take action that sets compassion apart as an emotion.

Compassion allows us to experience other emotions such as forgiveness and also leads us to 'give back' in life.

Compassion, however, has a balance point, feeling too much can be as bad for us as feeling too little. Have you ever heard the term 'compassion fatigue' used for those who work among suffering? It's used by our minds to protect ourselves from the emotional impact of what we're witnessing. This can be conscious or sub-conscious and is a recognised medical condition. In today's modern era of constant images being bombarded at us on media, it's becoming more common in the general population. We're less able to feel compassion if we're constantly surrounded by images of suffering.

Compassion demands that we take appropriate long-term action. Rather than fixing a short term problem it's better to provide a long term solution. 'Give a man a fish, and he can feed his family for a day. Teach him to fish, and he can feed them for a lifetime.'

Forgiveness

'Forgiveness is the attitude of the strong.' —*Mahatma Gandhi*

The more I think about it, the more I feel that forgiveness is one of the most important things we can do in life. I forgive easily, but I'm also aware enough to realise and understand why I forgive.

Why do we forgive? Because it allows us to break free from destructive emotions such as resentment, anger, and pain and it gives us the capacity to let things go and have closure, which is good for our health. It's important to let go of all the bad thoughts and emotions. They're in the past and dwelling on them is not healthy. Forgiving and moving on is important for our well-being and is healing for our body, mind, and spirit.

Forgiveness helps us achieve our goals and become better people with healthier relationships. It benefits others as well as ourselves. We have less anxiety and stress and higher self-esteem. Imagine if no-one ever forgave anyone else? Our minds would become breeding grounds for all those negative emotions to grow. The world would be full of hate. Relationships would cease to exist. I can't imagine wanting to live in a world like that.

OK here's a thought. How can we forgive others if we haven't already forgiven ourselves? We don't need any external acknowledgment that it's OK to be able to forgive ourselves. This is an opportunity to do some soul searching. Is there anything in our past that causes us guilt or shame? The reason behind that guilt or shame is only based on our perception of what happened. Our negative reaction is only to our perception. If we can take responsibility for a bad choice or decision then we can start to put it right or accept accountability for it. If that means making an apology, then what are we waiting for? We should apologise. When that's done, let it go and move on. Forgive ourselves, love ourselves, and accept all our faults and weaknesses. In other words be self-aware and life really is better.

If someone has done us harm or spoken badly of us now is the time to forgive that person before grudges and ill will take over our lives. Resentment has been shown to make us feel ill therefore forgiveness should make us feel better. Let's just do it, forgive all the people that have done us wrong in the past and feel lighter and uplifted as a result.

There are many ways we can help ourselves to forgive. It can seem hard to do to leave resentment behind but eventually, it happens if we persevere. We need to remind ourselves of the harm resentment can do not just to others but ourselves and remember that forgiveness increases our spirituality. It's not enough just to think about forgiveness we need to act on it. If we feel badly about someone, we can actively try to speak well of them. We can use self-awareness to try to get to the bottom of our feelings, understand what triggered the resentment. We can ask ourselves whether we're being objective when we look at it or are we applying false assumptions?

'To err is human, to forgive, divine.' Alexander Pope said that but we don't actually have to be divine to forgive, and we are all human, so we make mistakes. When others make mistakes, we should forgive them.

Gratitude

'As we express our gratitude, we must never forget that the highest appreciation is not to utter words, but to live by them.' —John F. Kennedy

Gratitude has been described as 'the parent of all virtues.' It's the state of feeling or being thankful. I'm sure we can remember a time when we expressed real gratitude for a gift or help we've received. We should all be able to find something to be grateful for. Family, friends, our health, our minds, our emotions, the world we live in, nature's beauty, and my personal favorites good books and smart phones. I believe that just saying thank you whenever it's earned is a big step. It's a small thing to do but can have a huge impact on the one who receives it.

There are many benefits we can gain from gratitude. Emotional benefits include feeling good and being more relaxed, being more resilient, and feeling less envious of others. The Personal benefits are that we become less materialistic, more optimistic, and less self-centered and we have increased self-esteem. Social benefits mean that we're kinder, we have more friends, and we form deeper relationships with people. Health benefits include improved sleep and increased energy levels, and we also experience less sickness. There are also career benefits such as better management skills, networking, achievement, decision making, and productivity. I'm grateful every day but my sleep never improves, why is that?

Feeling grateful is associated with less frequent negative emotions and being energised and alert as well as being more enthusiastic about life. With all those benefits why wouldn't we feel grateful? It doesn't take any energy or effort on our part, and it's certainly not hard to do. Specific acts of gratitude have a variety of responses, but if we're generally more grateful, we become more spiritual, more agreeable, and less self-centered.

People who are naturally grateful display certain character traits such as having an increased feeling of closeness in relationships and admiration for the good qualities of others. They're frequently in a good mood and are happier and have strong feelings of social support. They're also less stressed.

Are we happier because we're grateful or are we more grateful because we are happy? Believe it or not, someone has actually studied this, but the answer is still elusive. The outcome is the same regardless. We should strive to be both happy and grateful. While everyone gets the benefits from being thankful, those benefits will be different for each of us.

Expression of emotions

'Art leads to a more profound concept of life, because art itself is a profound expression of feeling. The artist is born, and art is the expression of his overflowing soul. Because his soul is rich, he cares comparatively little about the superficial necessities of the material world; he sublimates the pressure of material affairs in an artistic experience.' —Hans Hofmann

If we have no outlet for bad emotions they grow, fester and become destructive. If we don't let out the good emotions, we'll lose out on the benefits and so will others around us. Feelings and emotions are not meant to be bottled up, they're like a can of soda, when we shake them up, they just want to escape, and if we don't let them, they explode. Expressing emotion is our safety valve.

Expressing our feelings can be a double-edged sword where negative emotions are concerned. I personally time box bad emotions, so I don't get the chance to overdo it. It's perfectly OK to give ourselves permission to feel negative emotion such as sadness or anger, but we need to limit the impact by saying 'I'll be angry for the next hour, but then I'll let it go and get on with my life so it can't impact me anymore!'.

We can express ourselves and our feelings through creativity not just talk. Write, paint, design, build anything to get those emotions out. Be violent about it if you have to, scribble and scrawl over the paper, slapping some modeling clay about works wonders particularly for anger (I speak from experience on that one) it's amazing how like flesh the clay feels! OK, that's just creepy!

By being aware of bad emotions, it'll help us to be able to cope with them. Expressing emotion can be an indicator of intimacy with others as its part of open communication and dialogue. We can open up much more to someone we're close to, but we need to beware of abusing that trust!

Summary of emotional self-awareness

In summary, I'll end this section with some positive actions we can take to help us manage our emotions and help with our journey to self-awareness. Some of them are very general, but you may just find that they work.

- **Regular exercise.** (Not again!) This releases reward and pleasure chemicals in the brain, which make us feel better. Being fit also makes us healthier, which helps in managing emotions.
- **Being kind to others**. Because thinking of others helps us stop worrying about ourselves.
- **Be open and accept whatever happens to us.** We should learn to appreciate what's happening and always avoid criticism of others or situations.

- **Communicate well.** We can spend time with other people and enjoy their company and be open and honest in expressing our feelings.
- **Distract ourselves.** Yes, we really are that shallow. Watching a bit of TV, reading, or surfing the internet will probably help us forget that we're feeling down.
- **No negative thoughts.** If we find ourselves having bad thoughts, then we should challenge them by looking for evidence against them, and replace them with good thoughts.
- **Spend time outside.** Being in the fresh air, especially around nature, is very helpful for calming emotions. There's evidence that we need to see horizons, so if we can climb up a hill and look at the view, then we should.
- **Be grateful.** Thanking people in person for doing nice things for us, and remembering it helps us as well.
- **Play to our strengths.** This often means doing things that we enjoy, but it also involves doing things that are good for us.
- **Notice the good things in our lives.** In other words, count our blessings.

Forgive with all our hearts and be grateful for everything. Love with passion and laugh with enthusiasm. Hope for the future and be optimistic about the outcome.

Emotions are important, and it pays to be aware of our own and others' feelings. Highly emotionally intelligent people do this all the time. Like any other, it is a skill that can be developed and which is well worth acquiring.

Chapter 3

PERSONAL DEVELOPMENT

*'Education is the great engine of personal development. It is through
education that the daughter of a peasant can become a doctor,
that the son of a mineworker can become the head of the mine,
that a child of farm workers can become the president of a great nation.
It is what we make out of what we have, not what we are given,
that separates one person from another.' —Nelson Mandela*

Introduction to developing our personal skills

What is personal development?

Personal = One's own, belonging to us.
Development = the action of becoming larger, fuller, more mature
or organised.

I think that says it all. This belongs to each of us personally and only
we can define what development we need or want in various areas of our
lives in order to become more mature and organised.

In order to embrace personal development, we have to be able to deal
with change. We have to understand the change and find opportunities
with it. We have to be open-minded about it and not make assumptions.
We also need to embrace the emotions that come with it and take
responsibility for whatever happens as a result. Both change and emotion

have been previously covered in this book and underpin our ability to be self-aware.

There's so much I could have included in this section but I've chosen to limit myself to a few key tools and techniques and some personal insights that may help us with our drive to be more mature and become more successful.

Work-life balance

'Don't confuse having a career with having a life.' —*Hilary Clinton*

Work-life balance is defined as 'Meaningful daily achievement and enjoyment that enriches us in all four life areas: work, family, friends and self.'

There is not an equal balance, but we can't have one side without the other. It's also constantly changing on a daily basis and is always going to be different for each of us. Because the balance fluctuates, we need to regularly think about it, reassess our position and tweak it where necessary. The balance at the weekend will naturally be different to that during the working week but the week as a whole should have balance. We have to allocate an amount of our precious time to work, but we need to remember we work to live, not live to work. Work-life balance is all about our ability to control and reduce stress. Stress in our lives is on the increase across the developed world, and any help we can get to reduce it should be gratefully received.

We have to remember that work is important for our self-esteem and helps to ensure we fulfill our values in life. The happiest people are not people who don't have a care in the world; those people are bored. The happiest people tend to be busy people, but they don't feel as though they're rushed off their feet. In other words, they have balance in their lives.

We should regularly ask ourselves 'what's the most important thing for me to do right now?' We can't do it all, and everything is not equally important. Most people get 80 per cent of their results, and therefore benefits, from 20 per cent of the work they do, so focus on the 20 per cent. You may have heard of the 80/20 rule before. Just because something is urgent doesn't mean it's important and just because it's important doesn't mean it's urgent. Urgent tasks demand our immediate attention, but we don't actually have to give them that attention. It may not matter if we ignore them. Important tasks matter and not doing them may have serious consequences. The urgency and importance of a particular task will change over time, so regular checks and reassessment of priorities are good to do.

Unfortunately, there's no magic formula for achieving a balance between work and life, but there are some things we can all do that will help.

Step away from email. Don't check it too often. I'm guilty of this. My smart phone is physically attached to me, and I'm constantly checking every app. Facebook, Twitter, email, messenger, Skype, the news the weather. Even though I have notifications turned on, I still need to look and check. I also need to remember that incessant checking of email and social media just adds to stress, not productivity. I'll learn. Just give me more time.

We can make people wait. That sounds counterproductive but if we make it clear to people exactly when we'll respond, 'I'll reply to your email within one or two days' not immediately and then stick to it, we'll be seen to be reliable, and do what we said we would. People won't mind, and they'll come to trust us. Our word is what people will judge us by. I'm very good at this, making people wait for things, but I do make sure I never let anyone down. If I promise to return an answer by a certain time I always do it but it may not be immediately.

Embrace the 'off' button. Leave our phone behind (No way! OK I struggle with this one!). Unplug and step back, get a perspective on life and gain the freedom to analyse it and so become less emotional. This is a serious example of 'do as I say, not as I do.' I'm addicted to my smart phone and would almost certainly require counseling if I were to give it up. At least I'm self-aware enough to recognise this as a weakness.

Just say no. We often say yes out of guilt or a false sense of obligation. We don't want to be perceived as letting people down. If we normally say 'yes' right away, we should stop, don't answer immediately, think about it and if we still want to say 'yes' then fine. We're saying 'yes' from a position of self-awareness. Don't justify saying 'no' or make excuses for it; we have a right to say 'no' if we want to. Understand what really matters, time is our most valuable commodity so don't waste it. Don't be a martyr by overworking. Being a martyr can make us feel good and powerful, busy even, but it's infuriating to others. By doing so we're really only asking for their approval. If that sounds harsh, it's meant to be. Our level of commitment has nothing to do with the amount we accomplish. Think back to the 80/20 rule. If we only ever commit to doing the 20 per cent, we will still accomplish 80 per cent of what we need to do.

How can we work smarter not harder?

This is all about ways to be more efficient with the time we have.

- **Prioritisation.** We all have a list of tasks we need to do. If you're like me, it's several lists. Allow a certain amount of time per task but focus for that time. The maximum time to sustain a good level of concentration is only ninety minutes then we need to change task even if it's unfinished. Move on to the next priority task.

- **Ease off the adrenaline.** Hopping madly from task to task makes us no fun to be around. We will crash mentally and end up achieving nothing. Running around like a headless chicken only makes us a headless chicken, not an efficient human being. Time management and prioritisation are tools that really help with reducing this behaviour.

- **Track time.** We should be aware of, know and understand how we spend it, for both work and leisure. Then we can decide, from a position of awareness, what's necessary and what satisfies us. What are our patterns? We all fall into them accidentally and should try to find ways to avoid them. Patterns become habit and habit isn't a good reason to do anything. If it's not a recurring priority task then it's done because we always do it, it's an addiction. Because we always do it isn't an indication that it's a priority. Be aware of time conflicts between work and life and plan to avoid them or manage them.

- **Manage our time.** We should learn to cut out or delegate what we don't enjoy or can't handle. Organise tasks and do what needs to be done, and then let the rest go. (time management is another topic later on)

- **Make a list** (or as I've said several in my case). Plan in order to stay focused. We can't let ourselves be sucked into other people's plans as it'll almost certainly cause our own plans to fail. Anxiety is reduced by the feeling of control. (Well this is me, the control freak, what else was I going to say?)

- **Forget perfection.** Good v fabulous? Be aware that what we're doing may not be perfect, but it's probably good enough. Perfection builds extra pressure on us when we're already stressed and except in a very few case, brain surgery maybe, it's unnecessary. Think progress, not perfection.

- **Leave work for work hours.** If when we finish work, there're jobs not completed we need to make a note of them, and then stop. Take a slow breath and acknowledge that we've stopped work.

Make a conscious decision to separate work time and personal time. Make work our friend; we enjoy it, even love it, so we should treat it well. We don't want to come to hate it. It's not the enemy. We wouldn't treat a friend or loved one badly so don't treat work badly. If we work long hours the work we do at the tail end won't be good quality.

- **Set our own rules**. We can ignore the 'you should do...' people, including me, and rely on our own intuition. We need to pace ourselves; there are times to throttle up and times to throttle down. Self-awareness is crucial for this.

We need to make time for fun. Positive emotions help us solve problems. Circle back to the previous section for a list of these. We should also take time for us, just ten to twenty minutes a day. This increases energy and our ability to cope. I use this time to meditate and maybe renew my motivation. This time shouldn't be used for work, family or friends only for ourselves.

Key work-life balance messages. If I had to sum this up in a few simple lines, it would be this:

Control and planning (well it would be coming from me!).
Don't listen to anyone else about what's important for you. Be self-aware.
We can do anything once we stop trying to do everything.
It's the quality of the time we spend that's important, not the quantity.

Time management

'Since time is the one immaterial object we cannot influence – neither speed up nor slow down, add to nor diminish – it is an imponderably valuable gift.' —*Maya Angelou*

Let me just say upfront that I'm not naturally a good time manager. I've had to work hard for this to become second nature to me. I'm good at it now, thanks to an overabundance of lists and my natural tendency towards being a control freak. It will never come naturally to me, and it's usually spoiled by my addiction to smart phones.

Time management is our ability to be aware of problems we have with our time and to apply tools and techniques to solve those problems. In a nutshell, if we're time poor this is a way to get our lives back. This can apply equally to our personal lives or our work lives. I prefer to think of my time as a whole and apply these techniques across the board to get a balance that works for me. Time management is not a difficult concept to understand however it can be surprisingly hard to put into practice, and it can take time. I recognise that's a contradiction and I'm afraid I can't help with resolving that one.

There are some basic rules for good time management. Organise everything into keep, give away, and throw away. This means every area of our lives, work space, head space, home, task lists and email. Apply this principle across the board. Don't procrastinate. We need to act and do it now otherwise, we never will. Make decisions now, or things will sit there forever. Prioritise what has to be done and what has to be done now, applying the urgent v important principle. Plan to use task lists and prioritisation (I love a good plan). Delegate, or give it away. If we're time poor, we don't have to do it ourselves. If we can find someone else who can and will that's great. I know that's easily said but not so easily achieved as it involves giving up some control.

It's easy to make basic mistakes which prevent us from applying effective time management skills. Not having to do lists means we'll forget tasks. We can't forget if they're on a list. Not setting goals means targets will be missed. This means we'll lose the trust of others and we won't be able to reward ourselves when targets are met. Not managing distractions means some of them, that are regular occurrences that we can manage, will be OK. Others that are surprise attacks will need us to put plans in place to manage them efficiently. Taking on too much causes stress and can undo all the good work done with lists and priorities. We should just learn to say no. Despite popular opinion multitasking isn't a good idea, it's an inefficient use of time. Sometimes it works, often it doesn't, but it's always a risk. Not taking breaks means we can't function at our best. Breaks are important; they give us a chance to breathe. If the maximum concentration time for quality is ninety minutes, it makes sense to take a break every ninety minutes at least.

There are lots of tools that can help us with time management. Activity logs help us keep a note of what we do, how long it took us, how we felt about it and its value. Everything that needs action at some point in the future is an input to these lists, i.e. emails, memos, events and reading material. We often try to carry all this stuff around in our heads. It all competes for attention, and some will inevitably get lost. Apparently, we can only remember seven things at any one time, and I can guarantee we all have more than seven things on our lists. After a list is complete, look back and analyse it. Ditch tasks that aren't productive, delegate where we can, reschedule tasks to a better time of day, look at how often we switch tasks. Include breaks as tasks and time for ourselves, this allows us to become more efficient. To do lists are much like activity logs but for tasks, we haven't done yet. Estimate the time for each task and breakdown those longer than ninety minutes into smaller tasks. These tasks should also be prioritised. Organisation is important. We can spend the first fifteen to thirty minutes of each day making or re-ordering our to-do lists in order to increase our efficiency. Use a diary or calendar to schedule tasks and check and adjust it regularly. Rewarding ourselves if we do well improves our motivation. Managing our email effectively means dealing with it first thing in the morning every day. We can even schedule a task to do it. If the item is actionable, action it, do it now if it's quick, delegate it if possible or defer it for later action. I have no unread emails in any of my inboxes, and I have a lot of inboxes.

Going through this process, or one similar, helps us feel in control (it shouldn't come as a surprise that I'm happy with that) no matter how busy we are. It makes us feel more productive, focused and less stressed. Here's a thought, 'Technology gives us more time to be busier.' Technology is not the answer, it's just another tool. We should manage our time, or it will manage us! There's a brilliant analogy out there for time management which is worth repeating here. Rocks, pebbles, and sand. It's repeated commonly on the internet in various different ways, you may have seen an alternative story with the same message.

Rocks, pebbles, sand

A teacher smiled to his class as he began the lesson. He held up a large, empty glass bowl into which he carefully placed a selection of large rocks until they reached the brim. He asked the class if they thought the bowl was full. They all nodded in agreement. The teacher smiled again and started putting smaller pebbles into the bowl until they too reached the brim. He shook the bowl lightly and they settled into the larger open spaces between the rocks. He looked at the class and repeated the question, asking if the bowl was full. Feeling a bit uneasy now, the class again agreed it looked full. The teacher then poured sand into the bowl and shook it gently. The sand settled into all the remaining small spaces. Now the jar was full.

The teacher explained that the bowl represents life. The larger rocks are the things that should really matter to us, our family, the people we love, and our health. These are the things that would fill our lives even if everything else was gone. The pebbles represent the next priorities, such as our job, our house and our car. The sand is what fills the rest of our lives, it's the little things that shouldn't really matter to us. If the sand goes into the bowl first there's no room for the stuff that matters. If we spend too much time on the unimportant things, we'll have no time left for the important ones.

The moral of this story is to focus on those things that make us happy; they're our rocks. Make time for family and friends, eat well and exercise. Going to work, cleaning the house and fixing the car can always fill up any other spare time we may have. Take care of the important things first, and only look at the small stuff, the sand, if we've taken care of the big stuff, because it can easily fill up more time than we can comfortably give it. Focusing on setting our priorities is the message to take from this.

This story is short and sweet but oh so true. It's worth making a list (yes another list) of your rocks and pebbles at least and also some of the sand so that you recognise what stops you from dealing with your rocks.

'rocks, pebbles, sand.'

In summary time management means not keeping everything in your head. Use lists, diaries, and spreadsheets or whatever system works for you. It's about being specific about tasks and actions, not vague, so you know exactly what needs to be done. It means losing the big stuff, breaking it down into manageable tasks and prioritising them. If a task is too big, we will continue to put it off until it becomes so important it impacts everything else while we do it. It's about prioritisation.

Time management gives us back some control over our lives. It can sometimes take time to set up, but once it's up and running, then it's worth it to get our lives back. If you only remember one thing from this section make it Rocks, pebbles, and sand.

Self-confidence

'We gain strength, and courage, and confidence by each experience
in which we really stop to look fear in the face... we must do
that which we think we cannot.' —Eleanor Roosevelt

We'd all like to be more confident, right? It helps us manage our fears and makes us better able to tackle challenges and change. It increases our performance, happiness, and social ease as well as our health. I'm not naturally confident, but I've taught myself to be, in situations where I really need it.

Self-confident people have more time for friends and family, and they enjoy stronger relationships. They create positive results and become role models, and they don't suffer self-doubt. We can all put on a front and appear to be confident in certain situations, but beneath it all, we know that we're not and that self-doubt is what needs to change. I have to admit to still having self-doubt now and then. I think that's just human nature so I try to get over it.

Confidence impacts every area of our lives. It's more attractive than physical perfection (for those of you out there who are single and actively looking) but beware of coming across as over-confident or 'cocky.' That's not attractive. As with everything, there's a balance.

How do we go about improving our self-confidence? First off we fix the things we don't like about ourselves. These are the same things that came out in the self-awareness section so don't try to reinvent the wheel. Exercise is important (Ugh not again), we should play to our strengths and knowledge areas. We can all be confident when we're well within our own comfort zone and doing what we do well. Confidence has a snowball effect. As soon as we do something well our confidence increases and we achieve more. As a result, our confidence is boosted again. It doesn't matter where we start or how small the first step is, the snowball will soon become an avalanche.

Self-confidence is an important area of self-awareness. Self-confidence is having a strong sense of our own self-worth, and not relying on others for validation of our self. People with good self-confidence are more able to present themselves successfully and are often described as charismatic. They're prepared to voice unpopular opinions, and not always 'go with the flow.' They're also generally decisive; being able to make good decisions based on their own values not the opinion of others.

Self-confidence is vital for job performance, but it's also important for our personal lives. Without the ability to *'tell it like it is'* when necessary, and to stand up for the right thing, it's very hard to achieve anything, especially during tough times.

I can think of lots of things that help towards self-confidence. Having balance in our lives gives us time to think instead of worry. Self-esteem is important as we need to be able to like and love ourselves, recognise our strengths and talents and also having a positive attitude. When we feed our minds with good information we develop a more positive attitude and personality. We become more influential and persuasive with others and enjoy greater confidence and self-esteem. The old information technology expression GIGO meaning 'Garbage in, Garbage out' could also mean 'Good in, good out.' When we decide to eliminate bad thoughts and emotions we can start to bring about personal change. Like physical fitness, mental fitness takes training and practice.

In order to develop self-confidence, we need to concentrate on positive actions.

- **'Positive affirmation.'** This is speaking to ourselves positively saying things like 'I like myself.' A lot of our emotions are driven by the way we talk to ourselves and what we say. See the section on 'self-talk' earlier on.

- **'Positive visualisation.'** This is seeing our goals as already achieved. Creating a picture of what our success looks like and replaying it frequently. Some people create mood or vision boards for this.
- **Surrounding ourselves with 'Positive people.'** Happy, confident, optimistic people who are successful and whose outlook will influence us.
- **'Positive mental food.'** This is about reading books and articles that are inspirational and motivational and so feeding our minds with uplifting ideas that make us feel happy about ourselves.
- **'Positive development'** or committing to learning our whole life. This helps us grow and take control of our lives and increases the speed of our upward momentum
- **'Positive health.'** Be fit and healthy, eat and sleep well, we need to recharge our batteries regularly. Take regular exercise to feel happier.
- **'Positive expectations.'** We should expect to be successful, popular, achieve our goals.

Self-confidence can be improved through positive thinking and self-awareness (surprise!) The first step is to believe that we deserve to be confident. This is not as easy as it sounds but if you understand the previous sections where I've written about 'self-talk,' then that's the key to getting into the habit of praising ourselves until we believe it. We can also list out our strengths (Yeah more lists) and make sure to capture absolutely everything that we're proud of about ourselves. If our confidence starts to flag, we can pull out the list as a reminder, and it becomes our motivation. If we want to be more confident, then we can visualise ourselves as such. If we want we can call it daydreaming but in a focused way.

We should learn to accept compliments rather than fob them off thinking they're not justified. We can learn to accept them gracefully without even thinking about it. We're often our own worst enemies when thinking about ourselves; self-doubt is a killer for confidence,. We need to stop doing it. I'm still working on that one.

It's important for us to accept ourselves in order to accomplish what we want out of life. We can build on that self-acceptance in order to become more confident, enthusiastic and ultimately happy and self-aware. We should allow ourselves to make mistakes. If we try too hard that's a mistake; we're only human. We should also be aware of how to bounce back from it. We need to live in the present. I've said this a few times before. Let the past go; life doesn't happen there or in the future. Life is happening here and now. We need to get over past events using what we've learned about self-awareness and forgiveness.

We shouldn't compare ourselves to others. We're individual with different values and skills. There will always be people better and worse than us. We must be grateful for what we have. We should always be comfortable in our own skin not only what we look like but what's underneath as well. If we have any insecurities, we should deal with them. If we focus on others, then we lose focus on what we should be doing. A good friend of mine sent me that nugget when talking about a mutual friend who was losing focus and it's so true.

Having realistic goals is something I've touched on before. Becoming self-aware is just another reason to ensure our goals are achievable. We don't want to set ourselves up for failure.

Lastly, the one that crops up again and again, positive thinking. This is very important for all aspects of self-analysis. We cannot think negative thoughts without them impacting every area of our self-awareness.

Focus and concentration

'That's been one of my mantras — focus and simplicity. Simple can be harder than complex. You have to work hard to get your thinking clean to make it simple. But it's worth it in the end because once you get there, you can move mountains.' —*Steve Jobs*

Get organised and take control (there it is again, my personal favorite, control). It helps if we organise our personal space, desk or office, kitchen or bedroom, it doesn't matter. Make to-do lists (lots and lots of them if you're anything like me). In order to properly focus we need to manage our time but be sure to take breaks. This is a must if we don't want to burn out. Meditation really helps. See the earlier section under Spirituality. Control and lists, I'm in seventh heaven!

Focus is like your body, and stamina can be improved with workouts (luckily I don't have to visit the gym for these ones). Ready for more? Reading is my go-to way to increase focus and concentration but make sure it's a book you enjoy otherwise it doesn't really work. Don't procrastinate just do it whatever it is. Multitask less; I know we're always being told to learn to multitask, but it's counterproductive for focus and concentration. Avoid distractions, well this goes without saying. We need to stay motivated. We can go and re-read the section on motivation, and even if we can't focus for long periods to begin with we can keep trying and eventually it will come. However, bear in mind, as I said before, the optimum focus time is only 90 minutes then we should stop, or we won't be able to effectively take in what we're doing, and quality drops quickly.

You'll notice that by this section in the book most of the messages have already been given. This is because, as I said at the beginning, all of this is circular; it's a spider's web of ideas which all feed into and off of each other.

If we're human, then we're going to get distracted. Life distracts us and technology is probably the worst offender. Email, texts, and social media are capable of taking away our focus for hours at a time. Luckily there are ways we can train ourselves to be more focused.

Studies have shown that negative thoughts distract our brains because we tend to dwell on them whereas positive thoughts improve our ability to focus. We also need to be aware of the noise in our heads, our 'self talk', and try to remove it by exercise, meditation, and good practices.

Next time we meditate we can try and see how long we can sit still and focus just on our breathing without getting distracted. As I mentioned earlier, we spend a lot of our day focused on things completely out of our control, events that have happened in the past and events that might happen in the future. What a waste of energy that we could and should be productively using elsewhere to improve our lives now, in the present.

Pressure, stress, and anxiety are leading causes of poor focus and concentration. When we start to question our ability, we lose focus on the task. Our attention is like a spotlight, focused on a moment in time; it can be a narrow beam or a wide beam. It can be focused internally on our thoughts and emotions or externally on information coming to us from our senses. It can also be focused in time, past present or future. We need to learn to focus this beam of attention in the right place at the right time.

Self-awareness helps us monitor our focus as well as our thought. It's important to the success of our concentration. As in the previous section where I've talked about recognition of triggers for stress or bad thoughts and emotions we can use our self-awareness to recognise the triggers that distract us from our concentration. If we can recognise the triggers, we can be prepared for them. Adjusting our thoughts accordingly and refocusing back where it's needed.

Another analogy I've mentioned before is emotions being like a muscle. Concentration and focus are the same. If we practice and exercise this 'muscle,' it becomes stronger. Be aware though that just like a muscle it can suffer from fatigue. In order to train our concentration and focus without over-tiring it, we should focus on quality. In other words, only focus on a few things at any one time but make sure they're the highest priority ones. This requires us to simplify whatever we're doing by using time management and work-life balance. We can also learn endurance. This is the amount of time we can spend focused on one task before giving up. In between bouts of concentration we need to rest our minds just like we would our bodies. Gaining flexibility of our minds in order to maintain focus under pressure is a benefit. Our minds need to be able to deal with distractions without breaking. Meditation can help with this.

Communication

Communication is an essential part of our everyday lives. It's one of the most basic skills we can learn effectively. A breakdown in communication can be devastating and, unfortunately, it's all too common. Communication is defined as the imparting or exchanging of information by speaking, writing, or using some other medium. It's an interactive process for sending and receiving messages and involves both the sender and the receiver. In an ideal world, the message sent will be same as the one received, but that's rarely the case. Sending and receiving communication involves our thoughts and emotions, our needs and wants as well as the facts. Misunderstanding is easy.

Communication is simply the act of transferring information from one place to another, whether this be vocally, (talking), written (using printed or digital media such as books, magazines, websites or emails), visually (using logos, maps, charts or graphs) or non-verbally (using body language, gestures and the tone and pitch of voice).

Communication only works effectively if you have the skills to do it correctly. It's vital we get it right. A message is only successful when both parties understand it to mean the same thing.

To improve our chances of sending a successful message, we should be clear on what that message is. We should think about who's going to receive the message and what their current thinking is likely to be. If we understand the potential impact of our communication and try to think about any questions it's likely to raise then we stand a better chance of success.

As I said, communication can be verbal and non-verbal, but we tend to concentrate on the words. The words are only part of the understanding in verbal communication. The reaction of the person on the receiving end will also be influenced by the tone we use and our body language. These are equally if not more important. Body language can cover, posture, hand gestures, and facial expressions. Just as words can be adapted for the audience, so can our body language. We're all guilty of making subconscious decisions about people based on what we hear or see. We need to be aware that others will be doing the exact same thing to us.

If we put ourselves in the receiving position, listening skills are also part of communication. Active listening helps build trust, respect and influence yet it can be overlooked as a skill. We want people to listen to us, right? We should be prepared to listen to them as well. This doesn't just involve absorbing information. It's good if we can analyse others behaviour and look out for any hidden messages. Most important of all is confirming back that we've understood. We need to look as though we are listening. Make eye contact, don't fidget and have good open body language.

Think about what we do when we have a conversation with someone. If we hear something we want to respond to (assuming we don't just jump in and talk over them), we stop listening and start thinking about our reply. This is how important information gets missed. If we're thinking about our response, then we're not listening.

As you can see, we need interpersonal skills for face to face communication. If we have these tools at our disposal and use them, we can build rapport and empathy.

Barriers to effective communication.

The best way to ensure there are no barriers to our communication is to recognise them, understand how they impact effective communication and then to remove them. Potential barriers including noise, interruptions and distractions are avoidable. We can seek out quiet places for important conversations. Physical barriers are often avoidable too, barriers such as time and place. We can choose our location, including environment and we can set aside time. Both these types of barriers can decrease the effectiveness of the message getting across. Our attitude is important emotionally. If we show a lack of empathy, bad perception or stereotyping that can lead to negativity. Bad beliefs, bad relationships, culture and emotion all play a part as well. Poor listening is one of the most common barriers. We can listen at 500 words a minute but only talk at 125. So a lot of listening time is effectively free time which is distracting for us as the listener. As a result, we don't pay attention, we daydream and consequently lose the thread. Using the wrong method of communication can confuse the message. Often a combination of media is better than relying on just one. Body language is fifty five per cent of communication. It's non-verbal but non-verbal clues can be ambiguous.

None of these barriers are insurmountable, and most are easy to remove or prevent. By anticipating them and trying to avoid them, we can greatly increase the effectiveness and impact of our communication.

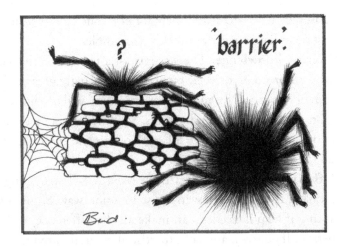

We all have to collaborate with others at some time. It's important to be aware of how our feelings and emotions and therefore our behaviour affects them. In order to have good, positive relationships with the people we interact with we should practice a few good behaviours.

- **Greeting people when we meet them.** By saying hello to those around us, and offering a warm welcome, we're setting the tone for positive and open communication.
- **Being approachable.** Giving off a friendly vibe indicates that we're interested in others and likely to be easy to deal with. To do this, smile, start conversations, answer questions positively and engage with other points of view.
- **Managing our mood.** Everyone has a bad day now and then. But shouting, criticising, and being aggressive only makes us look unapproachable. If we need to calm down after something hasn't gone exactly to plan, we can take a break and compose ourselves before talking with others again. Inconsistent behaviour leads to alienation. People won't want to risk being on the receiving end of our bad moods. If this does happen, put it right immediately with a genuine apology.
- **Saying sorry if it's warranted.** Following on from the above, if we've made a mistake or said the wrong thing, we should apologise for it. We shouldn't try to avoid any difficult or uncomfortable situations. This results in a build up of tension or bad feelings and

causes an awkward atmosphere for everyone else. Instead, resolve any potential conflict as quickly as possible.

- **Sharing knowledge.** The strength of a team, and this could be at work or home or even our family, is usually greater than the sum of its parts. This means that our 'team' will be able to achieve more together than as individuals. So, if we have something worth knowing, we should share this with others and encourage them to do the same with each other.

- **Offering help and advice.** If we see a friend struggling with a problem, we should try to assist in some way. Sometimes just asking if help is needed can make all the difference to the other person. If our own areas of expertise allow us to provide advice, or we're in a position to offer assistance, then we should do it. Our friend is unlikely to forget this help and will be more willing to return the favour when we're in a similar position.

- **Using our position constructively.** Valuing our friends is fundamental. However, this can't be achieved if we think we're always right. We're likely to be missing some valuable input, insight or ideas. We should always take the time to listen to other people's views and opinions, and consider them before making a decision. Fostering this kind of culture helps share the load, the responsibility, and the rewards.

- **Being sensitive to the moods of others.** Although it's preferable to leave problems at home, sometimes it's not that easy. If someone isn't doing well or is having a bad day, understand that there may be reasons behind this. Don't be quick to assume the worst; take the time to find out if there's anything we can do to help.

- **Thanking people for their hard work.** It's always good to thank people for any work that they've done for us, or that we've benefited from. However, if someone has gone the extra mile for us or we can see that they've put in considerable effort, we should be sure to offer praise and recognition, including a simple 'thank you.' Getting into the habit of expressing gratitude will help to improve people's attitudes towards us.

Success

Self-awareness, emotional awareness, and personal development are the keys to success, but not everyone sees success in the same way.

Decision + Focus + Consistency of Purpose = Success. It's not always the person with the most ability who succeeds but the one who wants it most.

Our decisions will determine the results in our lives. We have to decide what's really important to us ensuring we think about all the areas of our lives. It helps to make sure that our goals are S.M.A.R.T. specific, measurable, achievable, recorded and timed. Some people swear by vision boards of what they want their success to look like. Above all, we should believe in ourselves and our ability to make it happen. To some success is material, what we own or can buy, but to others it's about emotions, being happy and grateful. Most of us lie somewhere in the middle.

Part of being successful is the ability to turn problems into opportunities. Successful people view problems differently. They identify and seek to understand them. They're creative about the options available and potential solutions. They think about the goal when deciding what to do and they learn and get better at making those decisions.

I included this in the introduction, but it's worth repeating here. If you listen to studies, there are three things successful people do. They spend time getting to know themselves, self-awareness. They spend time improving themselves, personal development. They spend time sharing themselves, emotional awareness.

It has been said that it's not possible to be negative and successful. We can be negative and rich and have relationships but because we're constantly thinking about everything that's wrong with us we can't be successful. I'm not sure about that, but I'm happy to consider it as true.

As with most of the topics I've touched on, the important keys to success are self-awareness and positive thinking. People around us 'catch' our mood and either become positive or desire to be so. If positive thinking and self-awareness can improve relationships, make us healthier and happier, then it goes without saying that they can help bring us success as well. This only works if we act on our positive thoughts. It's not enough just to think them it has to really become part of us. We need to visualise our goals, make change happen and influence the world around us in order to achieve the success we want.

We should only use good words when thinking and talking. We should only entertain feelings of happiness, strength, and success in our awareness of ourselves. We should ignore bad thoughts and instead substitute them with constructive, happy thoughts. Every time a bad thought finds its way into our minds, we can immediately replace it with a good one. In our conversations, we can use words that evoke feelings and mental images of happiness and success. Before starting with any plan or action, we can visualise clearly in our minds its successful outcome. Reading at least one page of an inspirational book every day and watching movies that make us feel happy both help with our feelings of well-being. Minimizing the time we spend listening to the news and reading the newspapers will also minimize the impact that bad news has on us. Associating ourselves with people who think positively helps us. Always sitting and walking with our back straight improves our confidence. We should walk, swim or engage in some other physical activity as this helps to develop a more positive attitude. All these things can help contribute to our success.

Even if our situation is not as we would want it to be we need to ensure a positive mental attitude and act on it to influence things for the better. We're the ones in control of our lives so we should stop blaming external factors and other people and take responsibility for our own successes by being optimistic, grateful and avoiding negative people and thoughts. We should learn from our mistakes in order to grow and if we're positive we will attract like-minded positive people to us.

Emotional intelligence

'It is very important to understand that emotional intelligence is not the opposite of intelligence, it is not the triumph of heart over head – it is the unique intersection of both.' —David Caruso

This is where self-awareness ends up. Emotional intelligence was introduced in 1995 in a book of the same name by Daniel Goleman. It has since become a widely accepted tool in the understanding of individuals and organisations. Emotional Intelligence or EQ (as opposed to IQ) is the capacity of an individual to recognise their own and others emotions and use that information to guide their thoughts and behaviour. It is mostly used for leadership quality improvement but can be equally important in our personal lives. It's an important link using both brain and heart, IQ and EQ working together. It's social intelligence. In a nutshell, it's being smarter with feelings! I can't include everything there is on emotional intelligence in this book. There's a wealth of additional information out there if we want look into it in more depth.

Knowing our emotions

The ability to identify and be aware of our emotions is central to emotional intelligence. Goleman states that an inability to recognise emotions means that we're more likely to be adversely affected by them. In fact, self-awareness is the basis of Goleman's argument. The more aware we are of our emotions, the more likely we are to be able to make informed decisions about our life. This includes being always aware of certain things:

- How do we feel?
- How did we feel before, during and after a specific event?
- Is there a pattern to our emotional reactions?
- How do we feel about ourselves?
- How would someone else view our current situation?

Managing emotions

Having identified emotions, we can learn how to manage them effectively. Goleman suggests that this skill can be learned and developed. Without it, we're much more likely to feel out of control and unhappy. It's also useful when dealing with other people, particularly during disagreements. We can ask ourselves, 'Is the way we feel a hindrance or a help?' And 'Under what circumstances do we share our emotions with others?'

Motivating ourselves

The next step is to be able to control and draw on emotions to help achieve our goals. This is particularly important for our creativity. The other key emotional intelligence skill is self-control. Goleman states that it "underlies accomplishment of every sort." Points to consider when thinking about self-control include:

- What do we want and how can we get it? If we don't know what we want how can we ever find out how to get it?
- What's in our way? We can work hard to remove barriers to our success.
- What motivates us? The more we know this, the better chance we stand of staying the distance.
- How confident are we? If we aren't confident, we can work to build it up and thereby increase our chances of success.

Recognising emotions in others

Self-awareness can also help promote empathy (see previous section). Being able to understand how others feel and why is vital to most areas of life. Managing relationships in our personal life or in the workplace cannot be successful unless we understand individual motivations. So here are some questions to think about when trying to understand individual motivations:

- Why did a person act the way they did or say what they said? What was the real reason?
- Do people react to us in a consistent manner? What does their reaction tell us?
- Do we pay attention to non-verbal communication such as body language?

Handling relationships

Effective relationships require self-awareness and also emotional awareness. Both are covered earlier in the book. Having read those sections we can now ask ourselves:

- How do we influence others? What impact do we have?
- How well can we judge their reactions? Is our insight correct?
- Do we think about how we want people to feel? If we do, then we can have more fulfilled relationships.

In Goleman's original book the central message is that emotional intelligence is significant in determining our quality of life and our success. Goleman believes that too much emphasis has been placed on traditional measures of IQ; however, he does not see EQ and IQ as mutually exclusive but simply as different disciplines.

Self-awareness is the start of emotional intelligence, followed by self-management, social awareness, and relationship management. All of these are covered in this book.

When we're aware of our strengths and limits, we'll be more confident about what we can and cannot do. Self-confident people are more assertive about what they believe to be right. Being assertive doesn't mean we always get our way but rather that we put our thoughts and ideas across confidently and explain why we believe a particular decision or idea is the right one. We stand a much better chance of bringing people along with us, on the journey, if we do.

According to Daniel Goleman the competencies associated with self-awareness are:

- **Emotional self-awareness**: recognising our emotions and the impact they have on our life.
- **Self-awareness**: identifying our strengths and limitations.
- **Self-confidence**: knowing our self-worth and capabilities.

'What shadow do we cast? Followers want feelings of excitement, personal significance and to be part of a community, but above all they want leaders to be authentic. To use the best of you to deliver through others, you need to

know yourself and show yourself. Authenticity, self-management, humility, and courage are dimensions of character that when properly developed help leaders avoid derailment' (Goffee and Jones - 'Why should anyone follow you)

I love that quote; it's powerful. It means being seen to be open and honest at all times and applying it with integrity. This can be a big leap for some, impossible for others and a lesson I learned very early on. It always pays off in the end. It's all about our ability to understand and manage ourselves and our relationships by recognising and controlling our emotions and those of others.

'Be yourself with skill (Bill George, 'Finding Your True North') This book has some good messages, and in summary, they're very similar to those detailed in previous sections of this book.

- **Having a passion for our purpose.** People always notice our passion for things. How many times have you listened to someone and thought they were just going through the motions showing no passion for a subject at all.
- **Practicing our values.** Our values are who we are and who we want to be, if we don't live them, then it's all a lie.
- **Leading with our heart.** Integrity and honesty come from the heart and are born of emotion so we should let it lead us.
- **Developing connected relationships.** We should be fully connected and 'there' in our relationships, ready for open communication.
- **Having the self-discipline to get results.** Stay on our course in the face of challenges, pressures and distractions, focusing and concentrating on achieving our goals.

As you can see emotional intelligence pulls everything together from all the sections in the self-awareness and emotional awareness sections of this book.

So what does this mean? This means ensuring we are good at being ourselves and living our values. In fact ensuring we excel at it. With time this becomes second nature, after all, it should be easy to be good at being ourselves, so why do some people find it so hard? They always present the face they think others want to see, a mask to hide their true selves? Don't do it; we should always be ourselves and if we think our true self is not good enough, see the previous section on self-awareness and change it! Take our hearts or emotions into everything we do as it makes us much more genuine and dare I say human. Presenting a human face to the world gives us a big advantage over those who don't, can't or won't. Being authentic inspires and motivates both us and those around us to higher performance and success.

'The entire topic of a leader's ability to inspire subordinates comes down to the leader's willingness and ability to both be aware of and comfortable using emotion' (Zenger & Folkman)

Without an ability to recognise and use emotion comfortably we can't expect to help or influence others in a good way or expect them to listen to us in return.

The following list is traits seen in people who do not embrace emotional intelligence or who use emotion *'Without skill' (Lombardo and Eichinger)*

> They are self-centered, they don't relate well to others, they don't inspire or build talent, they are defensive or arrogant, they are too narrow-minded, and they don't deliver results.
>
> Do we want to be this type of person either at work or at home? I know I don't, and I suspect you don't either. I bet we can all recognise some of ourselves in those comments, at least some of the time though.

Emotional intelligence framework

In our interaction with other people, when we apply Emotional intelligence to our lives, we move from being centred on self to an inclusive relationship position.

The following are lists of behaviours commonly associated with what is called Red or Green behaviour and the potential impact it has. Red behaviour is the result of not applying emotional intelligence to relationships, and Green behaviour is when we embrace the use of emotion with the skill to recognise the impact it can have. If we even just skim a few examples we can clearly see the difference this can bring to our personal communication and relationships in all four areas of our lives, work, family, friends, and self. Life in the Green zone seems much easier and more comfortable doesn't it?

Red Behaviours:

We feel threatened and defensive

We use shame and accusations and blame others

We see others as the problem or enemy

We are rigid and reactive

We don't seek or value feedback from others

We don't listen effectively

We see conflict as a battle and seek to win at any cost

We communicate disapproval and therefore trigger defensiveness in others

Impact of Red behaviours:

Creates a low trust, high blame environment

There is an undertone of threat and fear

People are guarded and hostile

We see mistakes as failure and therefore avoid risk

We depend on external motivation

It creates anxiety and rivalry

It fosters a narrow perspective

Green behaviors:

We seek to respond non-defensively using persuasion rather than force

We look for solutions and take responsibility

We welcome feedback and talk calmly about difficult issues

We are interested in other points of view, and we listen well

We seek excellence rather than victory and look for the win-win

We seek deeper levels of understanding

We build mutual success

Impact of Green behaviours:

> Creates high trust, low blame atmosphere
> There is mutual support, communication and shared vision
> There is honesty and openness
> We see mistakes as learning
> We cooperate
> We are prepared to take risks
> There is friendly competition
> We take a broad perspective
> It creates excitement

The main lesson to be gained from the application of emotional intelligence to our interaction with other people is simply increased openness and awareness of others. Consider the following behaviours in the Red and Green zones when applied to this lesson.

> **Openness in the Red zone.** We distort reality or pretend to be what we are not. We're guarded and hidden behind a facade. We talk at a superficial level with no substance. We're unaware or unreceptive to verbal and non-verbal communication. We're insular and not inclusive
>
> **Openness in the Green zone.** We share our outlook willingly. We acknowledge and express our feelings. We recognise our intention knowingly and make decisions based on it. We fully consider feedback from others and learn our lessons in order to improve ourselves.
>
> **Awareness of others in the Red zone.** We ignore people and don't listen to what they have to say. We're quick to judge. We're not present mentally. We're oblivious to our personal impact on others
>
> **Awareness of others in the Green zone.** We acknowledge people and include them. We pick up on intention and feeling and act on what it tells us. We stay present and focused. We actively manage our personal impact on others.

It's obvious that the Green zone is where we should be aiming to be when interacting with other people but we should stop and think for a minute about where we really are. This is one of those times when we need to be honest with ourselves.

There are various levels of listening as we take the journey from the Red zone to the Green zone, this doesn't happen overnight, and there's no 'space transporter' to do it. It's another journey and our level of listening and interaction changes as a result.

> To begin with, we ignore the person talking; we're not present, and we don't listen.
>
> Then we lecture the person and judge what they say using phrases such as 'yes but,' 'you're wrong,' 'my problem is,' 'you think that's bad.' If you've been on the receiving end of this behaviour, you'll recognise that it triggers bad feelings.
>
> Later on, our conversation is at the task level, but at least we question and talk and interact with others.
>
> Finally, we recognise feelings, tone and body language. We help clarify by encouraging, empathising and reflecting back what we hear, see and feel. The positive impact of this Green behaviour is fully engaged and fulfilled relationships.

Once our journey to the Green zone is complete, we can still find ourselves facing situations which will have triggers that can put us back into the Red zone. So long as we think about what our personal triggers are, from our self-awareness, we can prepare for them and have avoidance techniques in place. Some of the common triggers to take us back from Green to Red are:

- Being treated unfairly (My personal big trigger)
- Feeling spoken down to and lack of respect
- Not feeling appreciated
- Not being listened to
- Someone else taking the credit for our work
- Being kept waiting
- Someone not delivering when they said they would

- Feeling criticised or blamed
- Unrealistic deadlines
- People who think they know it all

We should think about these triggers. We've all experienced and been on the receiving end of at least one of them, probably many. How did it make us feel? Look back at the first table and read the impact of Red behaviour. Does that sound familiar? Now look at the impact of Green behaviour on the second table. Wouldn't you rather be in that zone?

There are some things we should consider as we take this journey. Do we actively support people in taking care of themselves physically? Do we model these behaviours ourselves? Do we truly value, regularly recognise and express appreciation to those people we meet? Do we believe passionately in what we're doing? We need to move towards being able to answer 'yes' to all these questions.

There are further questions we can ask ourselves on the journey, particularly regarding our interaction with others and our relationships. Why is this relationship important? What difference would it make if we improve this relationship? What feelings do we have when interacting with this person? How do these feelings impact our interaction, well-being, and the relationship? How open are we in this relationship? What would happen if we were more open? What is stopping us from being more open? What could we do differently? What will we do differently? If we know the answers to these questions, then successful relationships are within our grasp.

Do we want to live in the Green zone? Do we want to break the cycle of Red behaviour for a particular relationship? If we do there are steps we can take to ensure it happens. Be brave and have the difficult conversations (apologise and listen). Employ brain to mouth buffering rather than blurting out the first thing that comes into our head. Consider our body language and what it says about us. Seek to understand the other person by applying empathy. Wipe the slate clean of previous bad interaction and start with a fresh approach. Remember we now have the emotional intelligence tools to look at this differently, but the other person may not have those tools. Realise that we can have a new lease of life in our relationship with a person even after things have gone wrong. I've had a chance to do exactly this recently, and I'm so grateful to have been given the opportunity to rebuild the relationship.

There are a wealth of books and references out there that can give us a more in-depth look at the psychology of emotional intelligence if that's what we're interested in. The information here should give us enough to be able to change the way we interact in relationships at home and work. The benefits are easy to see but just to recap:

- We can apply influence in our relationships
- We can use empathy with others
- We have emotional self-control
- We can do an accurate self-assessment of our behaviours and emotions
- We have self-confidence
- We have emotional and self-awareness
- We are motivated to succeed
- We have better social skills and therefore better relationships
- We can self-manage to be a better person
- We have reduced stress
- We have increased success.
- And loads more...

Why would we continue on in our work and personal relationships without applying these common sense principles? Try being emotionally intelligent and see how it makes a difference.

Summary of personal development

Self-awareness and emotional awareness are all about our minds and how we can train them to improve ourselves. This last section on personal development is more about action and applying tools and techniques to help us organise our lives and be better than we are.

Improving how we manage our time with work-life balance and time management is a big change and will allow us more productive time for the important 'stuff.' Remember Rocks, Pebbles, and Sand.

Confidence, focus, and concentration are topics all about being able to back up the lessons from self-awareness and emotional awareness so that we can be the best we can be. This then, leads to success and shows us how we can achieve it.

I've deliberately put the emotional intelligence section at the end as this really builds on all the other mental and physical skills to support it.

Afterthoughts

Writing this book has made me realise how much of this actually gets used in my life and how many times a day I actually, even if subconsciously, think about the messages I've just downloaded from my brain. I expected this for the personal development section, as I mentor young people on a regular basis. However, it came as a surprise when writing the self-awareness and emotional awareness sections how much more self-aware I am than I was, say, twenty five years ago and how much more open I am to sharing with others. Maybe some of the messages I've received, over the years, actually stuck and took root with me. After all, I've written this book and shared part of myself with you.

As I've mentioned somewhere in the text, probably creativity, I love art in all its forms. The illustrations in here are my own originals. As I brain dumped, my hands insisted I be creative in a different sort of way, just to mix it up a bit.

I hope you've found something in here that has at least made you think twice about your life in a positive way. If not I hope you enjoyed it anyway.

If you haven't already started on your journey of self-awareness, then all I can say is, 'just do it.' You can now understand the importance of emotions in defining your values and how you react, or not. You've got some tools for personal development which you can choose to apply, or not. It's always your choice how you use the information given to you, but I'm optimistic that at least some small part has stuck and taken root with you as well.

To say this has not been easy is the understatement of the year. I've sweated over the content, the words, what to include and what not to include, how to prioritise the information and how to present it effectively while trying not to send you to sleep. I've gone through the whole gambit of emotions in the process. I've been bored, angry, excited and passionate. I've laughed, cried, and been grateful for the help and support from friends and family. I know I've driven some of them mad in the process and I can only hope they find it in their hearts to forgive me, in the spirit of self-awareness of course.

I now have every respect for writers everywhere – you rock!

If you want to know more about me or the spider, Webstar, then please visit my website at www.authorjo.co.uk where you can also find a 'Contact me' page.

Acknowledgements

www.mindtools.com
www.psycholgytoday.com
www.au.reachout.com
www.selfcreation.com
www.pathwaytohappiness.com
www.verywell.com
www.change-managment-coach.com
www.skillsyouneed.com

Printed in the United States
By Bookmasters